W9-BUP-220

TEN
Dumb Things
Churches Do

He says people just disagree.
He says children just reject their parents' church.
A community that exemplifies the gospel in its
life together and its life in the world.

7 Pastor leaves you → you feel like a child/teen without your parent
→ relief → go back to old way
abandonment → get a new pastor ASAP
longing for what he was to you
real need → sick, married, lonely, dying

TEN
Dumb Things
Churches Do

And How
To Avoid
Them

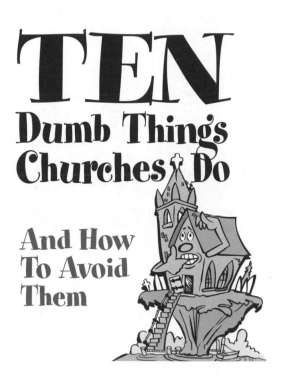

by
Philip Wiehe

MOREHOUSE PUBLISHING

Copyright © 2001 Philip Wiehe

Morehouse Publishing
P.O. Box 1321
Harrisburg, PA 17105

Morehouse Publishing is a division of The Morehouse Group.

All rights reserved. No part of this book may be reproduced or transmitted in any form or by any means, electronic or mechanical, including photocopying, recordings, or by any information storage and retrieval system, without written permission from the publisher.

Unless otherwise noted, Scripture texts are from (or adapted from) the New Revised Standard Version (NRSV) of the Bible, copyright 1989 by the Division of Christian Education of the National Council of Churches of Christ in the USA. Used by permission. All rights reserved.

Cover artwork by Larry D. Lerew.
Cover design by Laurie Westhafer.

Library of Congress Cataloging-in-Publication Data
Wiehe, Philip.
    Ten dumb things churches do and how to avoid them / Philip Wiehe.
        p. cm.
    ISBN 0-8192-1875.8 (alk. paper)
    1. Church management. I. Title.

BV652.W53 2001
254—dc21
                                                                    00-067873
Printed in the United States of America
    02 03 04 05 06 07 08 09   10 9 8 7 6 5 4 3 2

This book is dedicated to the many congregations with which I have been associated in the fifty-one years since I was baptized. Every one of them is truly a part of the body of Christ, and all of them have taught me something about my personal list of dumb things.

Acknowledgments

For the original inspiration for this book I would like to thank Glenn Holliman for providing excellent retreat spaces in which to work, I would like to thank Bill and the Reverend Meta Ellington for the use of their beach house and the Summit Camp and Conference Center for the use of Clark Cottage.

Thanks also to colleagues Claudia Earle, Bill Wrenn, the Reverend Ken Bradshaw, and Helen Clinert, who lent their particular expertise to the content. Special thanks go to my teachers and mentors in church consulting, Ruth Wright and Rod Reinecke. They provided not only expertise and time, but also encouragement and support. They have been in the trenches coping with the ten dumb things for a long time.

To engage in this kind of project at all takes the support of one's family that must put up with added disorder. Sean, Kristy, and Linda not only survived the disorder but also cheered the project on to the finish line. Thank you.

Most of all I want to thank my wife, the Reverend Linda McFadden. Linda's contribution to this book is enormous—from inspiration to editing—and this book is as much hers as it is mine. As colleagues in ministry, we have spent countless hours over the dinner table discussing ten times ten dumb things that churches do and what can be done about them. Much of the content of this book is derived from those conversations about the congregations we have been privileged to serve. I am blessed to live with, love, and be loved by a generous muse.

Contents

Sometimes churches act out of fear rather than trust.

Sometimes churches are confused whether or not to
act like a business.

Some churches have difficulty saying "no" to members
or staff.

Some churches do not engage in good planning.

Some churches have little idea what they want or
need for good decision-making processes.

Sometimes churches do not know who they are
or to what ministry God is calling them.

Some churches mishandle the time between pastorates.

Some churches do not honor the resources they have.

Some churches offer worship that is not consistent
with who they are or where they want to go.

Sometimes it is the pastor's fault.

Preface

This book is intended to be read by people of various Christian denominations. Since the book is largely about internal church issues, the reader needs to recognize that the particular personnel and processes discussed are similar from one denomination to another but may go by different names. The leading ordained person in a church may be the senior pastor, minister, or rector. The governing lay organization may be the session, board, council, or vestry. These terms are interchangeable except in instances where denominational polity or identity is an issue.

Also, there is a substantial divergence of language in our churches with regard to gender pronouns. As any good Episcopalian would do, I have taken a middle course in this matter. I tend to use inclusive language but am not slavish to the concept. I ask the reader to approach pronouns in the same manner as titles of the clergy: we are all a little different in our labels but the dumb things we do are the same.

Finally, regarding the dumb things churches do, I ask the reader to try not to be alarmed when your own church appears before you in the anecdotal material. What you may think is a precise description of your church is actually a composite of several churches that happen to look exactly like your church. It is my sincere hope that many readers from many different congregations will think that I am writing about their churches.

Introduction

Nearly every time I told someone I was writing a book entitled *Ten Dumb Things Churches Do*, the listener asked, "Only ten?" I usually replied that I was certain that there would be a sequel. Those of us who are locked in a love/hate relationship with the church often complain about the faults of the church including narrow-mindedness, bad management, and timidity. We also freely mock the sometimes silly and self-destructive behavior of this institution and its maddeningly slow response to change.

However, the Body of Christ endures by constantly forming and reforming. The people of the early church held clandestine worship in homes. Today in North America, there are churches in every neighborhood elbowing each other to compete in a context that is totally different from the first century in the Eastern Mediterranean. The Body of Christ has adapted to enormous changes in its environment. Artistic preferences are but one example. As the church emerged from persecution to union with the state, it adopted the architecture of the basilica where the state held its formal gatherings. Over the next fifteen hundred years, the solidity of Romanesque architecture, the heights of Gothic, and the order of baroque variously inspired people. Today some like to worship with classical music played on a pipe organ, while others like loud, contemporary guitar music, and still others prefer just plain silence.

Of course, there are differences deeper than artistic ones, such as scriptural interpretation, the relationship of church and government, creeds, doctrines, and just about everything human beings can think about and disagree about. So when Christians come together to be the Body of Christ, there are going to be some problems. If this were not the case, Saint Paul would not have needed to write all of those letters to his fledgling congregations.

Ten Dumb Things Churches Do

Over a period of two thousand years, we have developed an enormous amount of church procedure, some of which we zealously retain from generation to generation and some of which is discarded and replaced by each generation. This is the process of institutional formation. The process has been more than bumpy— at times it has been downright violent. Even in churches today, congregational meetings sometimes break down into fistfights.

In my more pessimistic moments, I have described the church as being akin to the *Titanic*. I am fairly certain that I am not the first person to do so. Probably if Saint Paul had known about the *Titanic*, he might have described one or more of his newly founded congregations in those terms. Everyone knows what happened to the *Titanic*—it sank. People are partly drawn to the story of the *Titanic*, I suppose, because of the irony in the statements by its owners and builders about its marvelous, unsinkable construction. The story is a good example of pride going before disaster.

So when we construct a simile such as "Fixing the church is like rearranging deck chairs on the *Titanic*," we have deepened that sense of irony because we know the fate of the ship. We could extend the analogy and suppose that the Episcopalians on the *Titanic*, when offered an opportunity to sing "Nearer My God to Thee" as the ship went down, would have deferred and organized a choir of men and boys. The Presbyterians, when informed of the imminent sinking, would have debated whether God planned the sinking and if the captain was doing God's will or not by ramming an iceberg. Members of the United Church of Christ and the Disciples of Christ would have organized a discussion group on the peace and justice issues surrounding the number of lifeboats and its effect on the people in first class compared with those in steerage. You get the point. While the church is going down, we appear to be fixated on minor if not irrelevant solutions to the real problem, which is survival.

Institutions undergo change all the time, some with glacial speed and some more rapidly. We can only hope that in the case of the church (here I am referring to congregations in the United States at the beginning of the twenty-first Century), there is a chance that the old institution will continue to repair itself from within and not sink. In my heart, however, I suspect that the church, as started by the apostles, will need to undergo some major changes to survive into the next millennium. Moving deck chairs on the *Titanic* won't help. Singing something other than "Nearer My God to Thee" will not make a significant difference. Patching the holes left by the iceberg will only delay the inevitable. In the end, we may need to start constructing a new form of transportation.

Having said that, I need to add hastily that I do not have any idea what a new form of transportation will look like. I suspect that small groups will continue to be the basic unit of the church. (Jesus probably chose twelve apostles because twelve is a good working number for groups requiring a high level of trust.) I suspect that owning real estate will have little to do with the church of the future. I suspect that clergy with multiple years of seminary training who are tied to large pension funds will be too expensive for most congregations. I believe that a good model for the future church is the Twelve-Step program: mostly small groups with a high trust level, a confessional ethic, and an action orientation. These small groups will embrace broad spiritual content but will have no professional leadership and no real estate—just the same familiar, welcoming format all over the world.

Ten Dumb Things Churches Do is not about making that new church from scratch. It is about taking the old church and retrofitting it to make it a viable institution for years to come. Some of the dumb things churches do are always going to be problems so long as the church is made up of human beings and not of furniture. So long as clergy are air-breathing mammals, some of them will make dreadful mistakes—like having an affair with a member of the staff. So long as church members have opposable thumbs, some of them will squabble over the color of the pastor's shoes. So long as children need to differentiate themselves from their parents, some (or most) of them will reject their parents' institutions, including the church. As long as people come together in congregations there will be differences among them. However, it is also true that when two or more are gathered in his name there will be the Body of Christ. There is good reason for hope.

This book is about making the system we call the local church one that truly reflects what we think the Body of Christ is supposed to be—a community that exemplifies the gospel through its life together and its life in the world. What makes this work so difficult is the fact that the church is unlike most other organizations in that its goals are abstract. A business is supposed to make money, the Red Cross is supposed to provide medical and relief services, and a symphony orchestra is supposed to make beautiful music. What exactly is a church supposed to do?

It is easy enough to say that the church is supposed to be the Body of Christ and is supposed to help bring about the kingdom of God, but what does that mean and how do you know when you have done even some of it? There is no way to completely remove the ambiguity, but there are a number of steps that laity and clergy can take to try to be clear about some things. This book is an attempt to state what can be done to convert what may be a vague purpose into something explicit. I have tried to bring about clarity in ministry by, first of all, naming dumb things that churches do. Naming the demons that inhabit a congregation is the essential first step in any process intended to exorcise them. Be forewarned, the demons will resist removal.

This book can be read by clergy, laity, or clergy and laity together (unless there is already a high level of distrust). It can be a "how to" book so long as the problem or problems are not causing hard divisions in your congregation. If your church is currently in conflict and your congregation does not have a good track record for resolving conflict, call a consultant or your denominational judicatory and get some professional help.

To say that the church does "dumb things" is not to say that I think the church is dumb. After all, we—you and I—are the church, and we do the dumb things. It is part of our nature to be imperfect; part of our task in life is to try to overcome or work around those imperfections.

At the very least, this book may help you understand what is happening in your midst while you wait for the lifeboats to be deployed. This book might even help you develop some strategies to avoid smacking into icebergs in the first place. Any time you have a sinking feeling about your congregation, check the horizon. If it is tilted, get to work. And pray.

God, grant me the serenity to accept the things I cannot change, the courage to change the things I can, and the wisdom to know the difference. Amen.

1 Fear

Sometimes churches act out
of fear rather than trust.

It is I; do not be afraid.
—John 6:20

S tuckwood Community Church, a middle-of-the-road
Protestant church in a town of ten thousand people, had an
aging membership. About one hundred people attended the
10:30 A.M. service, but there were no more than six to eight children
in the Sunday school. Tom Clayton, the new, thirty-something pastor, was called to the congregation because the search committee
wanted someone who could make the church grow. Tom was a
dynamic preacher and had demonstrated imagination and skill as
an assistant in a large church by starting several successful programs
for families within and beyond the parish.

After six months at Stuckwood, Tom felt he had a concept of
the dynamics of the town and of the congregation. Stuckwood was
surrounded by agricultural operations of various kinds that
employed Latino immigrants and migrant workers. Tom took a
crash course in Spanish and, with the help of a bilingual social
worker who was a member of the congregation, he offered a
Saturday evening worship service in Spanish. This new congregation started with only two or three families. Then one of the members of the little congregation brought his guitar-playing brother.
In a few weeks, there were ten families and some more musicians.
In six months, there were twenty Latino families—about eighty
people—worshiping on Saturday nights. The church council was
delighted, even though the new families were not major pledgers.

Then the Latino congregation asked Tom if they could move their worship to Sunday mornings. Tom thought it was a good idea; he also thought it might be time to add a part-time lay assistant, someone fluent in Spanish. It seemed to him a simple thing to move the 10:30 A.M. service to 11:00 A.M. and bring in the Spanish language service at 9:00 A.M. The church school held between services would be a wonderful cross-cultural mix.

Six months later, Tom was job hunting.

Sources of Fear

The Stuckwood congregation was afraid of something. Both individuals and institutions are reasonably fearful of anything that they think will hurt or diminish them, especially death. Congregations fear death. Fear of death may seem odd in a church that maintains that one of its favorite lines of Scripture is "Where, O death, is your sting?" (1 Cor. 15:55). We believe, supposedly, that we will attain the kingdom of God and be issued white robes washed in the blood of the Lamb—metaphorically, if not actually. We believe that the church is the bride of Christ and cannot die. Our earthly bodies die; likewise, earthly congregations die. Our souls go on and the church goes on. So, death, where is your sting? It preaches well but do we really believe it? What makes us so fearful?

Unlike Tom Clayton, pastors and laity alike assume that their responsibility is to keep the church going in the form of the particular congregation that they happen to be in at the moment. The church, of course, is not contained in that one congregation or in any one congregation. The church is not any one denomination. The church is not all of the mainline denominations or all of the free churches or all of the liturgical churches. The church is the body of all believers. No one—not even the Pope or the leaders of all the other churches—can change that. So let us cast out fear in the name of perfect love. Congregations and even denominations come and go. Whether we live or die, we belong to God. Death can and should be a noble part of life.

I want to concentrate on life, life without fear. What are some of the signs of life? In a church, signs of life might include the presence of many people on Sunday mornings as well as at the prayer group on Tuesday nights and at choir practice on Wednesdays. Normal attrition means that in order to keep these activities going, new participants must join. Even a flat growth curve requires recruiting and welcoming new members to replace those who are leaving or dying. This reality is a major source of fear. Pastors and laity are afraid that they will do something to cause people to stop coming to church, that is, to their church. Almost all churches talk about growth. Churches want more members because of the Great Commission: Jesus told us to bring in more members. (Of course, he actually said to "make disciples" and did not say anything about "members.") Sometimes we want more members so we can increase pledges to pay for repaving the parking lot. Unfortunately, while we may want and need new members, we also fear the changes they will bring.

Ask yourself this question: If you have a happy church of 1,000 members, what are you looking for in the 1,001st member? Is he or she a composite of the average person you have now? Would you prefer that 1,001 and 1,002 join the church as a married heterosexual couple about to have children? Is the 1,001st member of the same ethnic background as most of the current members? You can see where this is going. Fear rises in the presence of strangers. The more "strange," the more fear. Stuckwood Community Church wanted to grow—and did grow—but it ended up growing what felt like a tumor to some of the members. The new people were too ethnic, or too young, or too poor, or too evangelical. They had different ideas about worship, outreach, Christian education, and Bible study. The new people wanted to "take over." The situation did not seem "fair" to those who had been members for thirty years. The members fought. Some people left. The pastor resigned. The church ended up shrinking instead of growing.

It is a fact of biology that organisms resist invasive change. Our bodies resist attacking organisms such as viruses and bacteria by surrounding them with special cells. The church resists change in much the same way. Congregations surround the invasive newcomer with cells that will make sure the newcomers' new concepts do not infect the body.

It is also a fact of biology that successful species adapt to changes in their environment. While most of the dinosaurs failed to do this, humans have shown a marvelous ability to adapt to all kinds of changing conditions. We can change jobs, change governments, sometimes even change families, and continue to survive. Many of these changes are thrust upon us and we simply learn to cope. Changes are thrust upon congregations all the time, but institutional coping mechanisms are often calcified.

Our cities are littered with the shells of churches whose congregations moved to the suburbs. Sometimes the congregations rebuilt their edifices in the mushrooming neighborhoods. Sometimes they stayed put and became a congregation of rising average age until there were only a handful of elderly people left and the judicatory had no choice but to close the church. Sometimes the churches stayed and tried to adapt to their new environment, and some met with success.

The real estate is sometimes the biggest problem for churches. Consider for a moment Old First Church, an urban church built in the 1920s as a grand neo-Gothic monument for a well-off middle and upper middle class clientele. What motivated the leaders of that congregation to build their monumental fortress? They believed

- The church would grow and prosper.
- "If we build it they will come"—sort of evangelism-by-architecture (the inverse being equally important: "If we don't build it, they won't come").
- The congregation would always need the particular kind of interior space that lends itself to big liturgy—a big pipe organ, oak pews, and a large but remote pulpit.

However, many church clientele of the new millennium are urban dwellers more likely to prefer music generated on guitars, electric keyboards, and percussion instruments. They may expect improvisational preaching by someone who stands in their midst. They may want to get up and move around and find that the pews are in the way. These new congregations usually do not have the resources to maintain monumental architecture even if they could adapt it to their needs. They are more likely to rent a storefront or secure space in a local school.

Today, the board of First Church faces some difficult choices. They can sell the building and close down altogether, sell the building and rebuild elsewhere, stay where they are and completely change the focus of the ministry, or stay where they are—as they are—and slowly die, with or without dignity. All of these options are viable except dying without dignity. Death is okay. Trying again is okay. Relocating is okay. Ignoring reality is not okay.

Change happens. Fearing change cuts off life. I try to imagine what it would be like to travel back in time to 1920 and show the board of First Church what the latter part of the twentieth century would be like for their church. Armed with this knowledge, how would they spend their money? Would they still build monumental architecture? Would they build a more adaptable space? Would they reorder their priorities at all?

The real value of this exercise is to consider the board of First Church today as they face major decisions. What fears do they have? What assumptions are they making about the future? Are their assumptions based on an indefinite continuation of current conditions? If so, our learning curve as a species is not very great. We tend to think that if something works well now, it will always work.

Campus ministry has a lot to teach the church on this point. Campus ministry changes every semester as a new wave of students enter the system and others depart. New students bring different needs, ideas, and levels of energy. The program that was heavily subscribed one semester is a bomb the next. The reverse is also true. To say "We tried it and it didn't work" is almost pointless in campus ministry. One campus pastor of a large public university tried to organize service projects for years. Nothing worked. In the twelfth year, she had a very active program of service ministry.

In parish ministry change is slower, more subtle, and easier to resist. A group of people may well run the church for a generation or more, insuring continuity by handpicking and grooming their successors. The average age of the congregation may rise, but no one notices until there are only a handful of children in the Sunday school. The youth program dies because there are not any youth. A congregation like this one has a fear of change.

Consequences of Fear

One of the consequences of fear is a breakdown in clear communication. A church that is afraid of offending anyone will trivialize public communications. The thinking goes something like this: "We don't want anyone to leave our church. We certainly don't want anyone to leave our church because he or she was offended. So we will be careful not say anything in our church newsletter, service bulletin, sign board, or announcements that might offend anybody." Therefore, in order to be inclusive, we may say little of substance.

Efforts in the liberal churches to be inclusive are born in a genuine desire to treat all people with dignity and respect—love of neighbor. However, the result is often that congregations end up saying that anything and everything in the popular culture is okay. What the church says about itself and its identity as differentiated from the rest of the world is increasingly ambiguous.

In liberal Protestant churches there may be few boundaries and limits. Everyone is "in the community," regardless of their level of commitment. But if anyone slips away, it is a crisis. Newly called clergy are often bombarded with requests from well-meaning members to go and visit a disgruntled family. I have made some of those visits and caught an earful about either the previous pastor or the Christian education director or some member of the professional or volunteer staff. I recall only one instance when a family I had visited in these circumstances returned to the church to give it a second chance. Most did not come back because they felt they had already given the church plenty of second chances. They simply got to a place where they did not feel part of the church community—they may have been uncertain who was or was not a part of the community, or they did not fit in with the community culture as they saw it, or nobody listened to their ideas. At some point conversation stopped and they wandered away. It was easy to slide in; it was easy to slide out.

In a healthy church, communication flows smoothly among the pastor, the staff, and the members. In a not-so-healthy church motivated by fear, the only way to say something critical to the pastor is to complain to his or her spouse or a member of the staff. In this kind of church the only way to build coalitions on the vestry or board is to hold meetings in the parking lot with the right people. Congregations in which indirect or triangulated communications are the norm are congregations headed for or already in trouble.

Fear is usually somewhere behind all of the dumb things that churches do (and all of the dumb things people do). Fear of the ambiguities of the future can cause a congregation to fail to cope with changes in their context, resources, or sense of call. Fear of personal rejection can produce a failure to develop clear mechanisms for accountability, decision making, and conflict resolution. Each of these problems will be discussed in more detail in the next nine chapters.

What to Do about It

Fear of change is often at the heart of negative feelings about the church. When Jesus walked across the water, he told the disciples not to be afraid of the storm. If seeing is believing, then their trust in him should have removed some of their fear. Of course, Jesus rarely appears to us in this way. So overcoming fear takes trust, patience, and knowledge—"seeing" of a different kind. If we fear what we do not see or understand, then let us first try to understand what causes our fear. In the church that means looking thoroughly at the "what ifs": What if we made a change in the worship? What if we tried this new ministry? What if we made a plan to give away 25 percent of our income? Then, remember that our Lord walks beside us, even in a storm.

2 Business

Sometimes churches are confused whether or not to act like a business.

. . . for the children of this age are more shrewd in dealing with their own generation than are the children of light.
–Luke 16:8

"The church is run too much like a business." "The church is not run enough like a business." These two contradictory statements often turn up as complaints from the same vestry, board, session, council, or committee.[1] What is at the heart of these complaints? Let me begin with a story.

When I was a little boy, I wanted to be a doctor. More specifically, I wanted to be a surgeon. I had experienced some minor surgery and had seen films of surgical operations on television. What I knew about surgeons was that they used scalpels to cut into people and remove the offensive part. My father would play a little game with me. He would say, "My arm hurts, Doctor. What are you going to do?" "Cut it off," I would say. "My tummy hurts, Doctor. What are you going to do?" "Cut it out" was my practiced response. That is what I thought surgeons were supposed to do.

Sharp-Edged Discernment

Cutting is sometimes a part of healing. Knives and swords and scalpels are what we use to cut, divide, and separate. At birth, a knife cuts the umbilical cord and separates us from our mothers; in battle, a sword draws a line in the sand or inflicts a mortal wound. When a general surrenders to another general, he offers his sword as a symbol of military power. In Tolkein's *The Lord of the Rings*, as Aragorn assumed a position of power in Middle Earth, he wielded the sword Andúril that was reforged by elves.

When he said, "I have not come to bring peace, but a sword" (Matt. 10:34), Jesus was referring to a sword with a different purpose than Aragorn's. Jesus' sword separates good from evil. His is a sword that cuts off a person from his or her sinful past and divides that person's current values from former values. This is the sword that is "logos"—the Word that has come into the world. This is a sword of hard reality that makes hard decisions of the kind described in the hymn text: "Once to ev'ry man and nation comes the moment to decide / in the fight of truth with falsehood for the good or evil side." This kind of sword is the one described in Hebrews 4:12: "Indeed, the word of God is living and active, sharper than any two-edged sword, piercing until it divides soul from spirit, joints from marrow; it is able to judge the thoughts and intentions of the heart." The sword is the logos that has come into the world; the world has not been able to defeat it. So how is the sword of Jesus, the double-edged logos, to be used in the service of the church?

Now, at the dawn of the twenty-first century, concerned Christians need to exercise some sharp-edged discernment in order to be certain that there is a robust church in the twenty-second century. The game I played with my father comes to mind. For example, "The organist is breeding discontent, Doctor. What do I do?"

"Cut him out."

"The buildings and grounds committee cannot agree on whether or not to preserve the decaying steeple. What to do?"

"Cut it out."

"The minister is working eighty hours a week and his wife is threatening to leave him. What should he do?"

"Cut it out."

One parish rector was coming unhinged personally and engaging in a variety of inappropriate sexual behaviors. After exhaustive psychological testing, the priest was required by the bishop to resign from the parish and enter an extensive therapeutic program. Some members of the congregation accused the bishop of doing something "un-Christian." How did they get the idea that wielding the sword was un-Christian?

All of these wounds are symptoms of a church struggling with a potentially fatal disease: an inability to make clear-headed decisions that reflect the mission of the church. The primary symptom of the disease is fear that somebody will be offended by our actions. While disease can often be treated better with medication than with surgery, there are times when some swordplay or at least microsurgery is necessary. It is time for a call to arms—not only to defend the church from outside assaults—but also from decay within. This is not a new concept. All institutions must be deliberate about renewal in order to stay on the cutting edge.

In short, the dumb thing that churches do is sometimes to fail to act like a business when they should, and at other times to act like a business in ways and times when they should not.

While the wounds may be old, some new cuts may be required to generate healing. Somehow, we got the idea that saying "no" to dysfunction is un-Christian.

This chapter is about the church as a business. Has anyone in your church ever made the statement, "This church ought to be run more like a business"? What did he or she mean by that? The title of this chapter is ambiguous because churches err on both sides of the issue. In short, the dumb thing that churches do is sometimes to fail to act like a business when they should, and at other times to act like a business in ways and times when they should not.

Consider the case of St. Swithin's-in-the-Swamp—a lowly Episcopal congregation that is the whipping post for church critics. At St. Swithin's, the organist's alcoholism is a chronic problem. She is sometimes late to rehearsals, is rarely sober, and lately has smelled of alcohol even on Sunday mornings. There is always someone in the choir who can step in and conduct or play the organ. Choir members are accustomed to covering for their friend, who has been a member of the church for twenty years. No one wants to confront the problem. Removing the woman from her post, or threatening to do so unless she dries out, will make the choir unhappy. Furthermore, the organist does the job for very little pay, so there is no money in the budget to pay someone what the job is really worth. The problem continues.

The senior warden holds an impromptu meeting in the church parking lot one Sunday morning to review the problem of the organist. He intones, "This wouldn't be a problem if the church were run more like a business." What this comment reflects is the reality that in a business, chronically poor performance by a staff person usually results in dismissal. The speaker may desire to wield the sword, but others on the vestry fear that doing so may be "un-Christian." After all, people suppose that the woman drinks because she is unhappy and no one wants to add to her unhappiness. "The organist is such a dear soul for doing the job for low pay. It is her gift to the church. What would she do if she couldn't play the organ?" So her inappropriate behavior is "forgiven," which makes the vestry feel virtuous. In this church, an ethic of blanket forgiveness is greater than the ethic of accountability. The sword is sheathed. The alcoholic is not confronted. The church stumbles on.

What if the church were run like a business? How is a business run? More wisdom from my father: "The business of a business is to make money." There is admittedly a little more to it than that. Truly successful businesses also hold their own particular core values that influence all of their decisions. These values may range from an emphasis on customer service to innovative product design.[2] A successful business that makes money has a process for making decisions. The process may be as simple as "the boss decides" or it may involve a more complicated consensus of senior management. Either path depends upon having some clearcut criteria to use in making a decision. A very important criterion for any business in the long run is, of course, "the bottom line." How will the decision affect the company's ability to make money? The company needs to make money so that the owners can derive a living from it today, all the while maintaining the organization to make money for the owners of tomorrow. When the owners see a part of the business losing money, they may say, "Let's cut our losses." Then management takes steps to remove or alter the part of the business that does not contribute to the bottom line. Sometimes "cutting the losses" means cutting the staff. This is invariably painful, just like surgery. It is hard to cut something off without pain. However, if a business fails to cut its losses, it will eventually die and neither owners nor employees will have any income.

For the sake of comparison, let us look at a business, an airline called "Plane Wings Airlines," "PWA" for short. (There is no intention here to debate the merits of capitalism vis-à-vis Christian ethics. We will assume that PWA, Inc., is operated by enlightened capitalists who might even be members of St. Swithin's—perhaps someone like you.) Suppose one of PWA's routes is unprofitable. If you drop the route, there will be complaints from the people who depend on that route as well as the employees who are paid to operate that route. If you keep the route, you will make less money for the company. If you are also one of the principal stockholders, by continuing to operate this route you are making less money for yourself and for the other stockholders. This is a difficult decision because the welfare of many people is involved, but you are accountable to the board of directors and to the other stockholders to make the right choice. The directors want to see the company make money today and in the years to come. So, you wield your sword, cut off the unprofitable route, do your best to relocate staff, provide generous severance packages for the rest, and that is it. The stockholders are pleased. The company survives. There is accountability along the chain of command to the ultimate owners of the business, the stockholders. Money is leverage. If the company does not make money, the stockholders do not receive dividends. If the stockholders do not receive dividends, they will surely change management until they do. While decisions that involve an ethical issue as well as the "bottom line" are difficult, the path of accountability and the ultimate criteria are straightforward.

IBM was in the news some years ago because it had gone quickly from being a bellwether American corporation to being just another computer company. The principal reason for the huge losses at IBM was that the company did not anticipate the change in the way computers would be used in the workplace. Businesses wanted PCs that could be put together in a network instead of mainframe computers. IBM did not adjust to the changing market; other companies did. So IBM laid off tens of thousands of employees and cut whole sections of its business. Its

directors hoped that the cuts would return the company to prof-
itability and they were right. The successful business responds to
changing situations and makes adjustments.

Nevertheless, in the church we have a hard time making clearcut decisions, especially when those decisions involve changes that
we fear. Furthermore, it is hard to be business-like when we are not
clear what the business of the church really is. Consequently, we
have a difficulty saying what we would do if we did run the church
like a business. We need to bring the sword of logos into play here
to divide marrow from bone, fact from fantasy. I offer three areas
of ambiguity about the "business of the church."

1. We are not sure what we are selling. → Service to others, → salvation of self

Suppose that our make-believe airline, PWA, has an advertising
campaign that suggests that the airline is selling comfortable seats,
fine food and wine, and personal attention from a well-trained
staff. These are parts of the airline's service. Of course, PWA is
really selling transportation. PWA may use these elements as
enticements to sell transportation service, but in the end, a successful airline operates safely and on time. All the advertising in
the world will not overcome repeated news accounts of plane
crashes. Fine food and wine are wonderful add-ons, but they will
not take the passenger where he or she is going.

If the church is a business, what is the product? (Some may
think it crude even to advance this question. But if we are going to
get to the core of what it means to run the church like a business,
we had better be able to make a fair comparison with known and
understood businesses.) I submit that the church offers a unique
product in the form of a service called "ministry." Of course, different people in different congregations and different denominations emphasize one type of ministry over another. Some people
and congregations focus on the Great Commission ("Go . . . and
make disciples . . ." [Matt. 28:19]) as the core of their ministry.
Their bottom line can be measured in the number of people they
"bring to the Lord." Others might focus on programs for adults
and youth as the essence of their ministry; they measure success
by the number of participants in the programs. Another church
might focus on its worship and measure success by the number of
people in attendance or even on the artistic quality of the music
and other worship elements. Still others might emphasize preach-

ing, or running a soup kitchen, or simply maintaining a quiet space in which to meditate. A church can offer any number of services under the heading of ministry, just as the airline can offer any number of routes that are all transportation. The church that does something other than ministry is in something other than the church business. The airline that does something other than air transportation is in something other than the airline business. In either setting, the product must generate some positive result or a positive "bottom line." The problem is that in the church, some aspects of ministry may be quantifiable while others are not. This ambiguity is exacerbated by the fact that:

2. We are not sure what the bottom line is.

At PWA, the bottom line is net profit—the money left over after all the bills have been paid. Many church treasurers think of the church in much the same way. The church is doing well if there is some money left over after all the bills are paid. However, there is an important difference. The purpose of the airline is to make money for the owners by providing transportation to customers. The purpose of the church is to bring about the reign of God by promoting to its members salvation through Jesus Christ. Money has little or nothing to do with it.

Obviously, St. Swithin's-in-the-Swamp is not going to bring about the reign of God all by itself. Given the state of the world, the best St. Swithin's can hope for is a holding action while God engineers some miracles to bring about the reign of God. Perhaps this is a more realistic approach to the "bottom line" for the church, but it is still not easily quantifiable. In business, the bottom line is net profit, and satisfied customers—tangible, measurable items; but "the reign of God" is abstract. Can ministers presume to know for a certainty how God is working to extend the kingdom? It is very tempting to try to quantify the reign of God in the number of pledges, number of members, students in church school, and so on. This empirical data may relate to the reign of God, but there are plenty of situations where these measurements are useless. For example, a church in a stable neighborhood does not have to flog itself to continue expanding. Yes, they should approach new arrivals in the neighborhood. But the new arrivals may simply replace the members who die or move away. At some point in the growth of a church, it may be attracting all the members it can realistically attract, given competition from other churches and the demographics of the area. This means that rising costs have to be met by rising pledges or some other source of income, rather than by an increase in the number of pledges. In the case of an urban church, the reign of God might best be measured by the number of homeless people sheltered rather than by the number of members in the pews on Sunday morning. Quantitative measures aren't bad, but they must be used with caution. Similarly, qualitative measures aren't bad; but, like scores in figure skating, they are ultimately just someone's opinion.

Many churches attempt to express their bottom line in the form of a mission statement. The question is, how specific should a church be about its mission? Do we invoke high-minded phrases like "bring about the reign of God," or do we get down to cases and talk about administration of sacraments and housing the homeless? A highly specific mission statement gives clear direction to a congregation and its governing bodies, but needs to be revisited frequently as the talents and condition of the congregation change. An ambiguous mission statement requires church governing bodies to interpret and reinterpret as they make decisions regarding the expenditure of time, talent, or money. Specific or not, a mission statement is the way to make a church more like a business. If the church is run like a business, every member, every committee, and each staff person is evaluated on how well he or she adheres to the mission statement. In the same way, every employee of a business can be evaluated on whether or not he or she contributes to the net profit of the company. But how many committees of Christian education refer to their church's mission statement when choosing a curriculum? More to the point, how many churches have a coherent mission statement?

Potentially, the mission statement defines the bottom line. A properly drafted mission statement, whether specific or broad, is owned by the whole congregation. In theory, everyone has an opportunity to state what he or she believes God to be calling St. Swithin's to claim as its bottom line. If the church is to be run like a business, this then becomes the primary tool for evaluation and accountability. The members, paid and volunteer staff, and lay leaders of St. Swithin's are all accountable to each other and they are all accountable to God. The mission statement describes the bottom line accomplished by a product called ministry. We will discuss this further in chapter 4, along with strategic planning. There is still one more problem with the church as a business.

3. We are not sure what the assets are.

PWA has airplanes, hangars, maintenance equipment, and a head-quarters building with an expensive computer reservations system. The airline leases gates at airports and owns the rights to various routes. The directors consider these fixed assets to be essential for operating a quality airline.

The fixed assets of most churches include real estate in the form of church buildings, parish halls, classroom buildings, parking lots, and homes for the clergy. An amazing number of churches put pictures of their church on the front of their Sunday bulletins and stationery. A visitor from another world might get the impression that the congregation worships a building. Of course, not all churches have all of these assets. What is certain is that every church that has assets of real property spends a great deal of time and attention worrying about whether the furnace will last another year and determining how much money to put aside for future roof repair, if any. It is tempting to say that since the early church did not have property, the church of the twenty-first century need not have any. Such a sentiment is naïve and fatuous. We cannot simply go back to some idealized time or place in the past.

Nevertheless, the purpose of the church is not the ownership of property. In fact, this statement could be made about any business except the property business. People in business know this. When Sears began losing money, one of the first things the board of directors did was sell the fancy new Sears Building in Chicago. They did not leave the building. They leased back the space they wanted, but raised much-needed cash and made the company more flexible. It was not a time to be sentimental about owning a building. The purpose of Sears was and is to make money through retailing, which does not necessarily include owning a landmark property in Chicago.

It is difficult for us to change our perspective regarding church property because of hundreds of years of tradition. Since the time of Constantine, churches have had space that is dedicated to being sacred space. Therefore, this space is controlled, consecrated, and, usually, owned. Anything else is an "alternative" church. Property is not evil any more than money is. But property may well be the beam that we cannot get out of our eye. The assumptions that accompany property ownership badly distort our vision.

For example, the rector of St. Swithin's points out to the vestry that some churches rent out their property in order to generate income. The buildings and grounds committee gets to work and within a year, there are numerous building tenants. However, there are also issues. The Women's Fellowship that controls access to the Goodbody Reading Room is reluctant to rent to Alcoholics Anonymous. They resent the abundant cigarettes and coffee that go with AA meetings; and besides, Mrs. Goodbody (God rest her soul) was a teetotaler. On a separate occasion, the local housing association rented out the church to hold its annual meeting. Unfortunately it was a choir rehearsal night, so the choir was bent out of shape because they could not rehearse with the organ and had to settle for the out-of-tune piano in the parish hall. However, the gist of the choir's complaint to buildings and grounds was not about the inconvenience; rather, it was that the church was desecrated by permitting a secular organization to hold a meeting in it. The buildings and grounds committee was getting the idea that it would be easier just to keep the building closed.

The church that does rent out its space is a landlord. Someone, either paid staff or volunteer, has to manage the rental business. Insurance and fuel costs are rising and must be monitored. A custodian must clean the space, open and close the doors. Government agencies are watching churches to see if they are using their space for commercial gain that would make the activity taxable.

Some churches are on a historical registry, locked into an eternal quest to look exactly as they did in 1803, even if it costs buckets of money a year to make it so. (The magnificent cathedrals of Europe are great architectural legacies. Nevertheless, they are extremely expensive to maintain, and many of them would be completely empty if it weren't for tourists.) Every congregation needs to apply the cold steel of the sword when evaluating its property. All too often real estate, the principal fixed asset of the church, is a beautiful seductress that spends ever increasing amounts of the church's money in exchange for sixty minutes of pleasure once a week.

For just one scary moment, let us take a radical look at the church's approach to property and money. One can theoretically operate a church with little or no money at all. Who said there has to be professional clergy with a large pension assessment? Who said there has to be a church building to provide a space for worship once a week? None of these things are necessary to salvation, however, they can all be justified as contributing to salvation. Unfortunately, like any institution, the church is quicker to add what it needs than to shed what it no longer needs. What does the church today really need? What are the true assets of the church?

If the bottom line is salvation and not profit, then the "real" assets of the church are human talent and God's grace, not property. We have already noted that it is not necessary to have real estate to have a church. A congregation in Hawaii, for example, meets in the ruins of an abandoned church. Some churches rent community centers. Other churches have sold their property and rent back only what they need.

I am not advocating the dissolution of all church property. I am saying that our property sometimes blinds us to the possibilities of a more creative use of our physical assets. For commercial businesses, assets of all kinds are numbers on a piece of paper to be bought and sold as they are of use to the company. The church's key assets are our people and their spiritual gifts. To bring about the reign of God, there must be Christian people to do the ministry. So regarding our property, we must constantly ask ourselves, "How do our assets contribute to our bottom line?" Maybe, like Sears, we would be better off with less real estate. On the other hand, maybe, just by asking the question, we can be more creative in the use of our physical assets without clutching them in a death grip. Sound business practice means using the sword of discernment on all aspects of church life, including the use of the assets.

One more thought on people as assets: people are only assets in the context of the analogy with businesses. In business, people are customers, clients, consumers, or employees. Those terms do not actually apply to the members of a church any more than does the word "assets." New members are not commodities in a futures market. We have a problem when people are treated like consumers and not as partners in the church business. If the folk are *consumers* rather than people who share in the responsibility for making the enterprise go (that is, bringing about the reign of

God), then the task of staff and leadership is to please the consumers. Give Mrs. Goodbody the committee chair she wants and
she will pledge a bundle. Make worship a cheerful experience and
the plate giving will be up. Preach happy, entertaining sermons
and people will stick around and become pledgers. Sell peripheral
services such as day care and exercise classes and expand foot traf-
fic in the building. Pleasing consumer-members is a business
strategy that is, at best, tangential to the gospel of Jesus Christ.
Unfortunately, there is a trend to grow the church in spite of the
content of the faith.

What would happen if our airline, PWA, followed a practice
of simply trying to please customers regardless of the basic business strategy? Say management and advertising executives put
together a plan to give away champagne to every passenger on
every flight. Ads show a plane full of passengers being served bub-
bly and looking very happy. This is appealing—PWA soon has airplanes full of happy people drinking champagne. Unfortunately,
even though management put together a good deal on the purchase of the champagne, the promotion has caused problems in
other areas. The cabin attendants have their hands full circulating
with champagne bottles and have a hard time managing the rest
of their duties. Service is slow, flights are delayed, maintenance
suffers. Eventually, PWA has planes full of passengers drinking
champagne, but the planes and personnel are in such bad shape
that the planes never take off. Finally, the passengers figure out
that they are not going reach their destinations no matter how
pleasant the champagne. The passengers "deplane."

This is a rather extreme script. With any luck, PWA will spot
the problem early on when the first few complaints about poor
service emerge from people who do not drink champagne.

However, in the church, where we are confused about the
product, the bottom line, and the assets, we sometimes have a
hard time making even the simplest value judgments. St. Swithin's
membership committee figures it can increase attendance by
offering free lunch in the parking lot after the Sunday service. The
program attracts huge crowds as they fill the church to overflowing week after week. Unfortunately, getting these people to pledge,
teach Sunday school, or work in the soup kitchen is difficult. If the
goal is simply to have new warm bodies in the pews, then this kind
of promotion is a success. Program offerings such as childcare,

entertaining liturgy, and social opportunities are not bad, but they do not necessarily advance the reign of God. The dividing line between a fringe benefit and real product may be very thin. When does day care become ministry? When does performance liturgy become good worship? When does a church social event become Christian interaction? My point is that keeping people happy and busy does not necessarily advance the reign of God. There must be real product—transportation for the airline—ministry, salvation, and reconciliation for the church.

I began this chapter with a story that had the punch line, "Cut it out." Good "surgical cutting" is good decision making. It is bad medicine when churches fail to understand their own pathology to such an extent that they use the wrong knife to cut out the wrong thing, or more commonly, cut nothing at all. Operating the church like a business is beneficial if one is clear that the church is offering nothing less than salvation and the assets and energy required to bring about salvation. With clear criteria for making decisions, good decisions are more likely. Some of the decisions will mean saying "no" to one person and "yes" to another. In honest decision making there is pain caused by honest disagreements. However, if people on different sides of a decision recognize the one true Lord, then there is a built-in means of reconciliation, for our Lord commanded us to love one another (John 15:12). While a business of any kind can operate under this commandment, the church distinguishes itself from secular organizations by making love a top priority.

What to Do about It

Basically, replace ambiguity with clarity. The next three chapters are about particular areas of church life that are often fuzzy. Work towards being clear about:

- The purpose of the ministry
- The resources available to the ministry
- Communication about the ministry
- Responsibility and authority for the ministry

Also, do something very businesslike by evaluating at every opportunity. Each decision has consequences and only some of them can be predicted. A congregation, like any other system, improves only by constant evaluation. This means evaluating every meeting to determine if the decision-making process itself worked well in that meeting. Was everyone heard? Were there important contributions from particular members that should be affirmed? Did disruptive behavior or a poor agenda inhibit the work of the group? What might the group do differently at the next meeting? It takes some time to do a good evaluation, so the time needs to be allotted on the agenda at the beginning of the meeting for sufficient time to evaluate at the end.

To evaluate the work of the church, more and more congregations are engaging in regular mutual ministry reviews in which the staff and board (and sometimes the congregation as well) evaluate their own and each other's work in ministry. By placing problems out in the open, the leadership team can make adjustments in any area from the way the congregation handles simple decisions to the trajectory of the strategic plan itself.

This assumes most people are functional in an open style

3 Boundaries

Some churches have difficulty saying "no" to members or staff.

But speaking the truth in love, we must grow up in every way into him who is the head, into Christ.
–Ephesians 4:15

This chapter could have been part of the previous chapter on the church as a business. However, the problem of making clear decisions that result in saying "no" to someone is such an insidious problem in the church that it makes the top ten list of dumb things all by itself. In fact, I would say that the art of being the pastor of a congregation resides in being able to walk the fine line between being welcoming, positive, affirming, and all of those "Christian" things, while also being able to say a Christian "no." While the root "dumb thing" is the fear described in chapter 1, the principal manifestation of that fear is a failure to say "no" when "no" is what needs to be said.

This chapter presents a number of ways that the church fails to wield the sword that separates right from wrong, "yes" from "no." In every example, some person or group of persons chose to extend themselves in a way that diminished one or more other people: sometimes to build, sometimes to destroy, but always to gain power. There is a large cast of characters involved in the particular dumb thing of failing to say "no," but I will lump them into five categories: turf builders, wandering volunteers, pledge terrorists, antagonists, and addicts.

Turf Builders

A congregation employed a young woman as music director. Quite a talented musician, she could afford to work for very low pay since her husband was earning an excellent income. In her first year, she directed the adult choir and breathed new life into the moribund children's choir. She worked long hours well beyond her contract. At the end of the year, she asked for and received a pay raise based on the number of hours she was actually working. The next year she divided the children's choir into two age groups and added some special music events for the adults. Again, she ended up working about 25 percent more hours than she was paid to work. The board again rewarded her with a raise and the next year she added other choirs, and so on. After eight years, the music director had built a program that was easily the strongest in the church. A significant number of people had joined the church because of the program, and the music director had a salary that was only a little below that of the pastor. She was aggressive, to say the least, and brought about some liturgical changes through her powerful, handpicked worship committee. There was some tension between the music director and the pastor, but compromise kept them out of serious trouble.

Then there was something of a showdown. The right-leaning music director wanted to use the national anthem on a Sunday that coincided with the Fourth of July. The left-leaning pastor thought it was inappropriate. The music committee, the entire adult choir, and the parents of the children's choir members sided with the choir director. A handful of people sided with the pastor. The pastor lost. Not long after that incident, the pastor went on a sabbatical leave; in the next year, the pastor resigned. If that were the end of the story, one might conclude that the powers of church growth prevailed over the powers of political correctness. Unfortunately, not long after the new pastor arrived, the music director left because her husband was transferred out of town. The congregation blamed the new pastor for the departure of the music director. Actually, the real issue was the unresolved conflict about the propriety of the music director's empire. Major conflict erupted and many of the families who had joined the church because of the music minister left. It took many years to heal the wound.

At what point did this situation cease to be salvageable? Possibly, the situation was lost the first time that the board accepted the music director's self-proclaimed expanded job description by increasing her pay in exchange for increased time. Unless the music director had an agreement with the church that she could write her own job description, she was out-of-bounds early on. Many people perceived the music director's "extra" work as truly wonderful and generous. The program was successful in terms of numbers, but the program also generated a major division in the church when a turf war developed over control of worship. By the time the pastor drew a line in the sand, it was too late. The precedent of ambiguous or self-defined turf boundaries had already been set.

Here are some more examples. Most Episcopal churches built before 1970 have altars that attach to the back wall of the sanctuary. In this setup, the priest celebrates communion with his or her back to the people. Liturgical reform in the Episcopal Church throughout the 1960s, 1970s, and 1980s moved many of these altars away from the wall or added a table in the midst of the choir stalls or out in the nave. In this arrangement, the priest stands behind the altar facing the congregation. In Episcopal polity, the rector has sole discretion over how worship is done; even though thoughtful clergy may have prepared their congregations for a year or more for this major change, some people, predictably, didn't like it. The resistance sometimes manifested itself (and still does) in the behavior of the altar guilds, the groups of women who prepare and clean up around the altar every Sunday. In some instances, altar guilds refused to service the newly proposed freestanding altar, citing various reasons. Some complained that they did not have linen to fit the new table and could not afford to purchase any. I heard one altar guild member say that there simply was not enough time between services to move everything from the high altar to the free-standing altar or that it was just too hard. These complaints may be true; however, it was obvious in many cases that altar guilds were using "turf boundaries" to resist the change in worship to a freestanding altar.

In another example, Susan, a recent retiree, took all of the "official" church photos for her church. She photographed newcomers and placed their pictures on the bulletin board. She took pictures at parish events and special worship services. Susan was not a particularly skilled photographer and had only a modest camera. One Sunday morning, a few minutes before the start of worship, Susan asked the unsuspecting newly arrived pastor if she could take pictures during the new pastor's first worship service. The new pastor, who knew none of the history, said "yes," provided that she did not use a flash. Susan replied that she did not know how to turn off the flash on her camera and so would take no pictures. The pastor agreed to be available after the service to take any number of posed shots, but that didn't happen either. A few days later Susan went to the board of deacons and protested that she was being denied an opportunity to do the only ministry she knew how to do. The deacons backed her up on the principle that it was not Christian to deny this person her spiritual gift. Interestingly, the deacons were also responsible for the conduct of worship. They generally agreed that the taking of flash pictures during worship was disruptive. Some privately acknowledged to the pastor and to each other that for years they had wanted to tell Susan not to take pictures during worship. But the photographer staked out her turf and the deacons preferred to keep her happy rather than to do what they agreed was right concerning the propriety of worship. No one—not the pastor, the deacons, or the photographer—had the experience, courage, or clarity of thought to tell the truth in love in this situation. Susan continued to take pictures sporadically outside of worship, but constantly

---

The dumb thing that churches do is to permit
self-indulgent behavior in one instance and thereby create
a precedent to permit it in other instances.

---

poisoned the well by making it clear how unhappy she was. When did this situation get out of hand? The first time Susan was not challenged for taking flash pictures in the worship service. Since the incident was only the most blatant example of many instances of self-proclaimed authority in this congregation, it is not surprising that the situation had been out of hand for some time—few people actually like conflict. Most people would rather "forget the little stuff" than have a confrontation. But little stuff can lead to big stuff. The dumb thing that churches do is to permit self-indulgent behavior in one instance and thereby create a precedent to permit it in other instances.

A more subtle form of this behavior is illustrated by the person who perpetually takes the same position of responsibility in the church. He or she can carve out a territory by always being the chair of the buildings and grounds committee, the head usher, the president of the board, or just the person who assigns the choir robes. These people are self-proclaimed barons with a recognizable turf. If there is a lot of this behavior over time, the church can become a land of fiefdoms with barons swapping agreements on the management of the kingdom. The queen pastor is irrelevant and the peasant members are simply arms bearers in turf skirmishes: Christian education versus music, choir versus worship, women's guild versus missions committee. The battles may look like disputes over issues, but they are really disputes over territory. As the situation deteriorates, they become battles over personalities and end in a fight to the finish.

People who are otherwise good employees in their vocational lives and responsible spouses and parents in their family lives sometimes become petty tyrants in their church lives. This is not the place to explore the psychological and spiritual reasons why people behave this way; suffice it to say that they do. This insidious behavior is the bane of all not-for-profit organizations that depend on volunteer help. For example, empire-building professorial barons often control universities by volunteering for choice committee assignments and campaigning for faculty senate positions. By controlling several administrative committees, the bored art history professor can slide right into a deanship.

Usually the cause of the turf war problem is an inability to say an early "no" to some sort of inappropriate behavior. After the first time the photographer took flash pictures during worship, the pastor or lay leader should have said "no." Sometimes the altar guild has to be reminded that their territory does not include making decisions about worship. Personnel should have clearly written letters of agreement or contracts—it should be clear that the church will not pay for time spent doing tasks not in the contract. Businesses, unless they are start-ups or otherwise short-handed, usually define correctly the equation of work, time, and compensation. Churches, with ambiguous job descriptions for both paid and volunteer staff, often get these equations wrong.

Wandering Volunteers and Pledge Terrorists

Persuading people to do a volunteer job is the never-ending task of the pastor and of the lay leaders of a congregation. However, arm twisting is not the end of it. The recruited volunteer may then do any number of things: do the job badly, do the wrong job well, do no job at all, or some combination of these. Since we do not want to offend our members, we are reluctant to give any feedback other than positive feedback; consequently, a negative situation usually deteriorates. The volunteers wander around the church system sometimes organizing, sometimes disorganizing. The more we tell them what a good job they are doing, the more they feel affirmed and the more they continue doing whatever they are doing, for good or ill. What would happen if we were to give them a clear job description and accountability mechanism? We will discuss this further in chapter 8.

A particular problem is the volunteer who commits to a task and then does not do it. For example, the man who signs up for a Saturday of cutting the grass around the church and "forgets." While there are often good reasons for failure to follow through on a volunteer assignment, sometimes the failure is an attempt to gain a little power—"a passive-aggressive assertion."

By being passive, a person can draw attention to himself, even if it is not necessarily positive attention. Of course, in the church we are reluctant to do anything that isn't "affirming." So perhaps the head of buildings and grounds calls up the guy who missed his grass-cutting assignment. He reminds him that it was his turn and how important the job is. For a moment, the wayward volunteer has become an integral and vital part of the church team. Ironically, he may have been recruited for the job with the opposite message: "This isn't very hard and won't take very long." The subtext here is that the job is not important. How often do we signal our volunteers that what we are asking them to do is not important, "not much trouble," in order to persuade them to do the job? Is it any wonder, then, when they fail to follow through or attempt to make the job more important?

The fact remains that there are jobs to be done and not enough paid staff to do them. If the jobs are not done, the organization suffers. After recruiting, the next step is keeping volunteers from wandering away from the job. If we give our volunteers total freedom to do as they please—like Lone Rangers—we can expect them to ride off in all directions and eventually shoot at each other. While innovation and entrepreneurial spirit are important ingredients in bringing about the kingdom of God, gross inefficiency is not.

Related to contributions of time are contributions of money. It is not unheard of for a few of the top pledgers in a church to get together and hold their pledges hostage while they demand something from the pastor or governing board. This insidious behavior is usually one element in a serious conflict situation. People with a particular axe to grind choose to withhold their pledges while they sharpen their axes in public. Even after they have made whatever point they wanted to make, they often continue to withhold their pledges until they see what the board will do next, or what the interim pastor will do, or who the new pastor is, and so on. A pledge terrorist can always find a reason not to pay the pledge.

Pledge terrorists operate not only as individuals in opposition to the parish, but also as whole parishes in opposition to the judicatory. In either case, pledge hijacking is a thinly disguised political tactic in which what is supposed to be God's money is used as a weapon. Withholding a pledge, or significantly reducing the denominational asking, ultimately wounds the very community of which the pledge terrorist is allegedly a part. In Paul's concept of the Body of Christ, pledge hijacking is a case of the hand attacking the eye.

A variation on pledge hijacking is the terrorist disguised as a rescuer. In one pastoral-sized church, a well-off widow liked to bail out the church every year. The unstated arrangement was that the pastor was to call on this woman around November to ask her to cover the last month of the budget. In this way, the woman's rescue fantasy was fulfilled and the pastor got his December paycheck.

The only way to deal with a pledge terrorist is to just say "no." After all, pledging is ultimately a spiritual issue, not a tool for self-aggrandizement.

Antagonists

Without a doubt, the most destructive church terrorist is the antagonist. This character sees the church as his playground and he is the bully. By intimidation, he or she can control all of the comings and goings in the institution. They are a dumb thing unto themselves and have been properly exposed in Kenneth

Haugk's book, *Antagonists in the Church*.[3] His book should be required reading for all church leaders, clergy and lay.

In a program-sized church of moderately affluent, well-educated members, there lurked a particularly devious antagonist in the form of a Sunday school teacher who had been teaching for many years. She fondly referred to "her children," some of whom were now adults in their early twenties. She was a powerful woman, physically and emotionally. A box of tissues seemed to follow her about, as she was prone to weeping at the drop of a hat. She was apparently a good teacher, at least insofar as maintaining control of her classroom and showing up every Sunday with a lesson prepared. However, in her dealings with the other teachers she was something of a tyrant. One year she became head of the Christian education department, but that made her a target for criticism—a situation that she could not abide. She retreated to the classroom but managed to control the selection of the next Christian education leader. She was always assigned "her" classroom, because it was clear that any deviation from her orderly world would result in a flood of tears. Essentially, this woman controlled the Christian education department single-handedly and without any title.

Her power did not stop there. She could propose a project for her class that ultimately would demand the involvement of all the other classes. She would then propose that the project be brought into worship and the worship committee would give a green light regardless of whether or not the project had anything to do with the worship plan. In short, people had a hard time saying "no" to this woman. Anyone who did say "no" to her, for a good reason or not, would be in trouble. She knew everyone in the church as well as just about everyone in the small town; she spread rumors about those who would not bend to her will. The rumors were nearly complete fabrications, impossible to prove or disprove. She also manufactured and circulated rumors about the leadership of the church, both clergy and lay, just as a matter of course. She gained power by anyone else's loss of power. This went on and on until the woman took on the choir director over a music selection for worship. The choir director would not give up a planned choir anthem in favor of the Sunday school teacher's effort to have "her children" sing something during worship. The choir director had a lot of backbone and knew how to set limits. She said "no" and repeated it, again and again. She did not cave in to threats. The antagonist resigned and left the church, taking with her some teachers who were loyal to her.

While the antagonist in the story may seem extreme, she is all too common. The church abounds in such examples because the church frequently is a refuge for dysfunctional persons. For Haugk, the antagonist in the story would be categorized as a high-level antagonist who is dangerous to the organization. The turf builders of the first section would also fit into Haugk's categories, but as more benign sorts of antagonists. Both are common in churches, because somehow we got the notion that being Christian means tolerating everything, including inappropriate behavior. Sometimes members of a congregation will seek peace at any cost. In their daily lives the members must cope with all sorts of difficulties in their work and families, so they just want peace and quiet when they come to church.

Who can blame them? Church is supposed to be a sample of the kingdom of God to which we are all headed. Unfortunately, if a lot of energy is going into placating an antagonist, then a lot of energy is going into constructing the illusion that the situation is normal and acceptable. Surely, the kingdom of God is not built around illusion and lies. In the case of the tyrannical Sunday school teacher, the illusion was that she behaved in a normal way and that her demands were reasonable. People were afraid of her anger—expressed as fits of crying. Everyone from the pastor to the board to other Sunday school teachers were content to do what-ever it took to keep her happy. Consequently, the entire congrega-tion was regularly subjected to the woman's tyranny. From our perspective—distant from the situation—it is easy to see inequities. However, from inside an emotionally charged situa-tion, it is considerably more difficult to think clearly.

A methodology for coping with the antagonist can be sum-marized by saying, "Speak the truth in love." One must set clear boundaries and limits for these people and then stick to them, sometimes stating the limits over and over again.

Addicts

As an experienced Twelve-Step person, I try to avoid the tendency to see every problem as one of addiction or co-addiction. Nevertheless, the dynamics of the addictive family or the addictive system can be applied frequently to the church. Consistent failure to say "no" is a symptom of a dysfunctional addictive system that resembles individual and family patterns in addiction. Since many people in our society and in our churches have some experience at coping with addiction, either personally or with a loved one, this can be a helpful model for examining the dynamics of failing to say "no."

I once heard a wonderful analogy for the addictive system: an addictive system is like a maypole.[4] In another era, the maypole was a tall pole with a number of beautiful ribbons attached to the top. Girls in white dresses each held the other end of one fully extended ribbon. As the music played, the girls began an intricate dance around the pole that resulted in the weaving of a beautiful tapestry of interlaced ribbons. That multi-colored, woven fabric of ribbons represents the healthy system. The unhealthy or dysfunctional system in this analogy consists of the same maypole—but chains replace the ribbons. When the music begins, the people holding the ribbons have no choreography. Instead, they go wherever they feel like going—crashing and banging into each other. Eventually they are all standing next to the pole, wrapped in chains, unable to move. That is the addictive system. Each person can get out only by cutting his or her way out.

The chains that bind the participants to the pole are self-esteem and other needs and wants that can become hideously twisted out of shape in this set-up. In some way, the participants get something they need by staying in the system. For example, the turf builder who holds the same church job year after year receives some measure of self-esteem in exchange for his or her labor, whether it is good for the church or not. While any organization can become an addictive system, the church is especially vulnerable to this failing due to an inability to say "no."

Churches that are addictive in themselves are one or more of three types.[5]

In the first type, the pastor (or in a family-sized church, the matriarch or patriarch) is himself or herself addicted to a substance or to some destructive behavior such as rage. The most common example is the workaholic pastor. He is a person who cannot do enough for other people. He gets drunk on the affirmation he receives by working so hard attending all the committee meetings and doing all of the hospital visitations. He is happy when he makes someone else happy, but the euphoria has a short shelf life. He believes that he has the time and energy to please the women's prayer group, the buildings and grounds committee, and the parents of the children in the youth choir, even when these people have conflicting interests. One such pastor made a valiant effort to please all these groups with hard work. However, when his wife had a baby, she expected him to be home more. When he was not, things got nasty at home and people in the congregation took sides, sympathizing either with the pastor or with his spouse.

In another church, the pastor was addicted to rage. He had frequent displays of temper with the staff, coming very close to physical violence. The staff learned to tiptoe around the rector to avoid igniting his short fuse. (Anyone who has grown up in a family with an alcoholic will recognize these patterns of behavior.) The staff put a substantial amount of energy into placating the pastor so that he would not lash out. Under pressure, the pastor resigned dramatically right before Easter in the mistaken belief that the church would come begging for him to return, promising to be nicer to him. His ploy did not work, but the church was years in recovery. (A variation on this type of addictive system is contained in the story about the tyrannical Sunday school teacher in the section on antagonists.)

Another way that the church can behave like an addictive system is by holding whole groups of the usual players in an addictive system. For example, there may be several individuals or families in the church who never seem to like anything and complain openly and volubly about any- and everything. These disgruntled people can have everyone in the congregation thinking about them whenever a decision is at hand. In one such church, an unstated requirement for serving on the board of deacons was to have solid skills for enabling this kind of dysfunction to continue. The "codependents" were in charge of ministry. They wanted nothing for themselves and worked endlessly trying to please the unhappy members. Needless to say, their work was never done. There was massive low self-esteem in the congregation; the only people who ever joined the church and stayed more than a year were like-minded people. The congregation was truly chained to the maypole.

The third way the church can be an addictive system is by behaving like a substance that can be abused. In other words, the church itself becomes an addiction. In this case the dynamics of a particular institution mesh with deep unresolved needs of a significant portion of the congregation. A subtle version of this is the church that tries to make everyone happy on Sunday morning. If the music is loud and happy and the sermon is loud and happy, these people get their "happy pill" for the week. Other people get their high by being miserable. If the church can remind them that they are no-good, sinful wretches, then they may have the juice to mope through another week. They miss the part of the message about Jesus dying for their sins. For some other individuals, their role of "leadership" as an usher or committee chair may be the only affirmation they ever receive. These people are potential barons who need to stay in the system because it is the only one that accepts them.

Our churches have a lot of this dysfunction banging around, partly because mainline Christianity has such a hard time saying "no" to dysfunctional people. Somehow, the idea got loose that it is un-Christian and possibly un-American to deny people anything. We forget that sometimes loving one another means setting some limits with one another.

Before departing this topic, I want to examine one more dumb thing—the way that some people use the Bible to justify saying "yes" when they should say "no."

If you hunt around enough in the Bible, you can find a proof text for just about any activity: war or peace, drinking or abstinence, slavery or abolition, the banning or the acceptance of female clergy—just to name a few. One of the wonderful and amazing things about the Bible is that it holds little time bombs that explode in each new era. Our understandings about the impropriety of slavery and the role of women in the church are two frequently cited examples.

Reasonable people may disagree about the interpretation of any text. Still, when the interpretation of the text becomes the justification for behavior that corrodes the church, then there is something wrong with the interpretation. Consider the way we treat concepts of charity or, in Latin, caritas. Caritas is usually translated as either "love" or "charity," but our concepts of both of these words can get us into trouble. "Charity" can attach to itself a sense of pity, while "love" is such a large and complicated word that it lacks nuance. Perhaps a simple way to understand caritas is simply to look at the gospel.

The gospel is full of examples of Jesus' healing ministry, the stories he told, and things he said—all of which point to giving rather than receiving charity. The widow is blessed because she gave all that she had. Jesus said, "Turn the other cheek, " "Pick up your cross, " "Love your neighbor," and "Love your enemy." All of these passages, especially if taken out of context, suggest a kind of humility and total denial of self. Remarkably, we live in an era in which we have promoted the self to such to a high degree that these statements become truly radical. However, we miss the point when we use them to justify permissiveness rather than genuine *caritas*.

The story of the Good Samaritan is an illustration of this point. A man walking on the Jericho road is beaten and robbed. A priest and a Levite, who should have behaved better, walk right past the man. A man from Samaria comes to the injured traveler's aid and takes him to an inn. The Samaritan gives the innkeeper a substantial amount of money to take care of the injured man and promises to cover any additional costs.

While this is a story about charity, it is also a story about priests, Levites, and Samaritans. It is a powerful commentary on the religious leaders of the day and a warning not to dismiss Samaritans, who were despised for their worship practices (or possibly just for being different). This preaches well as a twenty-first-century sermon about diversity, but take a look at the picture it presents of charity.

I think of this story nearly every time I pass a hitchhiker by the side of the road. While the hitchhiker may not be beaten and robbed, he or she may have a story of hardship that would be the equivalent. But there is no way for me to know the story just by looking at the hitchhiker. We have all read accounts of hitchhikers who kidnapped the generous people who offered rides. Therefore, instead of risking personal injury, I drive by. I do not think my behavior is unreasonable in an urban society. I am able to say "no" because there is some real risk in saying "yes."

That is not the situation in the story. The Samaritan is not at risk in helping the injured man—although he might be late to his next appointment and his purse might be a bit lighter. Yet, the Samaritan's *caritas* is a model of no-strings-attached love that genuinely helps the receiver.

Where the interpretation of this and similar stories goes wrong is in using this kind of love to justify unbounded giving to people who keep taking. I have provided numerous examples of these people in this chapter: the tyrannical Sunday school teacher, the alcoholic music director, the workaholic pastor, the man who failed to cut the grass. These people do not just use the church— they use it up. They need to be loved, but we do not need to bind up their wounds again and again when the wounds are self-inflicted. The most loving thing we can do is to get them professional help and make it clear what we can and cannot do for them. If the Samaritan returned to the inn and discovered that the man he helped was still there, running up a lot of charges for room service, I hope that the Samaritan cut him off.

It is a serious mistake to believe that we can get personal Christian points by endlessly helping the same people again and again. That is not proper behavior for a church—it is behavior for a nursing home for the chronically deluded. The healthy church, on the other hand, can be a hospital where spiritually wounded people can receive genuine healing and be made whole.

What to Do about It

"Let your word be 'Yes, Yes' or 'No, No'; anything more than this comes from the evil one" (Matt. 5:37). The cast of characters presented in this chapter may or may not be from the evil one, but they can be steadily corrosive or explosively destructive.

- The wise pastor learns early on who in the parish is an empire builder and deals with him or her directly.
- Staff and lay leaders must be deliberate about setting limits on behaviors that are not consistent with the clearly stated goals and strategies for the ministry.
- Contracts for the staff and lay leaders provide a mechanism for keeping everyone on course.
- Regular evaluation based on those contracts is the key to enforcing the agreements.
- Highly disruptive situations require outside help (described in more detail in the conclusion of this book).
- Addictive systems can only be changed one person at a time.

4 The Plan

Some churches do not engage in good planning.

For no one can lay any foundation other than the one that has been laid; that foundation is Jesus Christ.
—1 Corinthians 3:11

Ah ha!

I grew up in the kind of family in which having a plan was essential. A common topic for dinner discussion was "the plan" for each of us or for all of us together. We were relentless about obtaining closure on "the plan" and regarded deviation from it as a serious breach. Asking my parents for permission to execute a plan that involved spending money was something like writing a grant proposal. Failure to have a plan was considered a weakness and was an invitation to ridicule. It has taken me years to figure out that planning does not come naturally to me, that whatever planning skills I possess come from my experience with my family. To my amazement, I have also discovered that not every family cares as much as mine did about having a plan and that churches, like families, are all over the map in their ability to plan. To complicate things further, God is constantly "making all things new," which may interfere with whatever plans a congregation has made. Planning for a church requires starting from the basics: the purpose of the church.

The Foundation of the Plan: The Mission Statement

It follows from the previous chapter that the purpose of a church is to be the Body of Christ and, by the grace of God, to bring about the kingdom or reign of God. However, if one posed the question, "What is the purpose of the church?" how many church members, church councils, vestries, sessions, worship committees, or buildings and grounds committees could come up with a coherent response? Some likely responses might be: "The purpose of the church is to teach the children about God." "The purpose of the church is to print the parish newsletter, to organize the annual bazaar, and to get through the Christmas season in one piece." We all know there is a deeper purpose, but we lose sight of it when we are down in the trenches doing what we hope is productive ministry.

All of us in the church business have days when we forget why we do what we do. I am not just talking about the bad days. On the good days, we may mistake our own glory for the glory of the One who died and rose again. On the bad days, we may mistake our job for that of a garbage collector. For better or worse, but almost always when we are busy at our labor, we may define the purpose of our work in narrow terms that relate to what we are doing at the moment. "The purpose of the church is to worship." "The purpose of the church is to be friendly to newcomers." Similarly, a pilot for PWA, the fictitious airline of chapter 2, may feel that the purpose of PWA is to fly airplanes while the ticket seller may feel that it is to sell tickets. They are both partly right. Both contribute to the greater goal of making money for PWA. They will not have jobs if they cannot help the airline make money. In the same way, a congregation has no reason to be if it cannot fulfill or at least engage in its mission.

In very basic terms, a particular congregation has no reason to be if it cannot be the Body of Christ in its particular time and place and cannot further the kingdom. The airline that fails in its basic task of making a profit by providing transportation soon goes out of business. However, the church is different. A congregation can fail in its basic mission to be the Body of Christ yet continue to exist for many years. Perhaps churches would be a lot clearer about their mission if, like a business, they were forced to close for failing to execute it.

Why the Mission May Be Unclear

Congregations often have a difficult time articulating their purpose. One reason for this ambiguity is that most congregations were founded by people who are no longer on the scene. In the life of an institution, that makes quite a difference. The founders had the vision and the zeal to create something out of nothing and to drive the institution forward. The next generation may see the institution as something they are obligated to pass on as it was passed to them. They may lack the motivation to engage in the kinds of risks that the founders were willing to take. If you are fortunate, there are members of your congregation who remember those adventurous days when you rented space in a restaurant and the entire Christian education program operated out of the back of a station wagon. Maybe some of your members can recall the excitement of rebuilding the church after a devastating fire. These kinds of memories help to keep the institution focused on its reason for being.

A more common reason for losing track of the purpose of the church is the fact that Christianity—especially mainline Protestantism—has been absorbed into the fabric of our North American culture. Jesus preached his gospel in a hostile environment. In Mark, Jesus constantly told the disciples not to tell anyone about him. He was subsequently executed and many others were persecuted for their beliefs. Most Christians today, however, are not subject to persecution for their beliefs; instead, they are the people in charge of everything from government to education to industry. In mainline churches the gospel, which contains the message that "the last shall be first," is being preached largely by people and to people who are the "first" and not the "last." One could argue that the church's "mission" has been accomplished, since Christian values permeate our society. However, it would be premature to beam up to the rapture because there is overwhelming evidence that sin and injustice still exist. Arriving at a robust sense of Christianity in which sin is a reality and Jesus Christ is understood as having died to reconcile us to God is not easy in a land that can explain almost every evil through psychology and sociology. The church does have a clear mission. We have only to express it and act upon it. Unfortunately, the mission is easier said than done.

The Mission Statement Trap

A congregation that was contemplating a capital campaign wisely organized some grassroots thinking about the future of the church. The pastor asked everyone to think about what the church would look like "if everything went God's way." While the question was provocative in that it pushed the congregation to look at the difference between where they were and where they thought God might be calling them, the question itself was preposterous. If everything went God's way, we would not need the church. Instead, we would all be issued bouquets of lilies and white robes and ordered to prepare for the imminent rapture. If everything went God's way, the church would be irrelevant. We need the church precisely because things do not go God's way. Sin abounds. On one hand, the Body of Christ is a defense against darkness and

---

No The dumb thing churches do about planning is to devote a lot of time and attention to the mission statement and then generate ministries strictly on the basis of the mission statement.

---

evil; on the other hand, the Body of Christ is on the offense, trying to bring about the day when the kingdom of God is upon us.

This statement about the nature of the Body of Christ derives from excellent sources such as Scripture, systematic theology, patristics, and probably the mission statement of the denomination. Such generalized statements about the Body of Christ are fine; and since Christians are working with the same basic sources, our mission statements end up looking much the same from one congregation to another. Nevertheless, a prosaic mission statement can be a trap.

Consider this example:

> *The congregation of Last Church-in-the-City is dedicated to telling the good news of the resurrected Christ by worship, study, outreach, and fellowship for people of all sorts and conditions . . .*

The dumb thing churches do about planning is to devote a lot of time and attention to the mission statement and then generate ministries strictly on the basis of the mission statement. That is like throwing a handful of gravel at a wall. All of the gravel will hit the target if the target is big enough. Is there a program that would *not* fit the above mission statement?

This is not to say that mission statements are dumb things. They are important reminders of who we are. The process that generated this mission statement for Last Church may well have been an all-day parish meeting or a weekend retreat. There may have been plenty of small group sessions that began by listing "what we like about Last Church, what we don't like, and what we would like to change." No doubt many pages of newsprint were devoted to brainstorming what the church will look like in five or ten years. Many creative ideas may have been put forward. However, when a congregation distills this information and actually writes a mission statement with which everyone can agree, it is likely to generate something bland like the statement above. The real benefit of the process was in the small groups—they may have had a lively discussion on the significance of "good news" as opposed to "gospel," "telling" as opposed to "enacting" the good news, "by" as opposed to "through" worship, study, and so on. Those semantic discussions are wonderful because they open up real issues about the purpose of the organization. The creativity that went into dreaming about the church of the future was quite possibly spirit-filled. The problem is that once the statement is homogenized to such an extent that no one finds anything objectionable in it, and then printed in black and white, it looks, sounds, and tastes bland. Worse, it looks, sounds, and tastes like the mission statement of the church next door, even though that church is a different size, has a different worship style, and is a member of a different denomination. The energy generated in the process that created the mission statement may be missing from the statement itself.

Suppose Hard Knocks Presbyterian Church has a mission statement like the one above. Further, suppose that they worked on their statement and proudly print it on the cover of their Sunday bulletin. A couple new to the community visits this church and wonders whether or not to join. They read the mission statement; they look at the brochure describing the church's program. The next week they go the Methodist church a few blocks away. They encounter a similar mission statement, program package, and worship scheme. They must then choose between these churches. Most likely they will make a decision based upon the time of the service, the friendliness of the greeters, the length of the sermon, or perhaps the size and vitality of the youth group. They are unlikely to select a church based upon its mission statement, no matter how well reasoned the mission statement may be.

The mission statement in and of itself is not a very useful tool for evangelism. The value of the mission statement is contained largely in the process required to create it—the interactive discussion about the purpose and function of the congregation. The mission statement also serves as a reminder to the congregation of who they are as determined by that conversation (which may not be all that different from the church next door). What is missing from this picture?

Consider the problem in marketplace terms. Imagine there are two bakeries in the same neighborhood. Both bakeries are devoted to making a profit for their owners by baking bread and pastry—that is the "mission" of both bakeries. However, one bakery employs a strategy of making the best possible products with the best possible ingredients. The other bakery is service oriented and has a drive-through facility as well as a place to sit and have coffee. As a consumer, you might go to one for your child's birthday cake and the other for a bagel in the middle of the morning. There is a need for both bakeries and enough business to support both. They have the same mission. They both succeed. But they have significantly different strategies for obtaining their results.

What is truly revealing about a congregation is probably not its mission statement. We all use much the same source material, and we are all allegedly heading toward the kingdom of God. Nevertheless, our congregations employ a wide variety of strategies to get there. Newcomers quickly figure out what is important to a congregation in their worship—whether it is the sermon, the

---

The dumbest thing a church can do in this regard is
to have a mission statement and no clarity about how
to execute it.

---

sacrament, the joyful noise, or the still small voice of God. A focus on one or more of those elements is fine. From clarity (or the lack of it) in worship, the newcomer may extrapolate clarity (or the lack of it) in the life of the congregation. For example, it may be evident from the content and aesthetics of the worship that the congregation is deeply involved in outreach programs in the neighborhood, or that it is dedicated to its youth ministry. The dumbest thing a church can do in this regard is to have a mission statement and no clarity about how to execute it. That is the mission statement trap.

When people whine that the church should be run more like a business, what they yearn for is often *clarity of purpose.* A lack of clarity creates many problems: needless announcements in the middle of worship, endless meetings that are as much social gatherings as work sessions, failed programs that refuse to be dead and buried, clergy and other staff working too hard at trying to do too many things, constant difficulty with pledging, and disengaged youth who cannot discern any reason to be a part of the mess.

A bakery unclear about its purpose might try to sell auto parts and become an example for the book *Ten Dumb Things Bakeries Do.* The church's product, however, is salvation by ministry, not croissants. God does the salvation and we do the ministry; the ministry is a subtle, complex, and even elusive product and service. It is essential that congregations be as specific as they can about what resources they will apply to particular individuals or groups in need and to what end—matters rarely covered in mission statements. The kingdom of God cannot be brought about by sheer force of human will. Saturation advertising on television may work when selling a box of cereal or a political candidate, but it is less successful for the kingdom of God. To "buy" the "kingdom" (not the one represented by a mouse with big ears), people must make faith decisions on their own, possibly inspired by things that happen in, to, and with their church community. People form such communities; the best thing that church professionals can do is to create an atmosphere in which a community may form.

The church is a tricky business. While it is possible to measure success empirically in the bakery by the amount of cash still around at the end of the day, there is no comparable statistic for the church. A congregation may go for years with no significant change in attendance, even though they have improved the quality of their faith, their life as community, and the neighborhood they serve. On the other hand, a congregation may be growing rapidly, but the reason that they are growing is that they serve free barbecue in the parking lot every Sunday.

The lesson that the congregation can take from the bakery is not about the bottom line—it is about strategizing with clarity. A

What are our gifts?

congregation must discern what its gifts are and use them well. A congregation must know its context and consider how best to minister within it.

Strategic Planning

A mission statement is a fine thing, but in the end mission statements are all much the same. The bakeries have the same basic mission statement as AT&T: to make money for the owners. However, their strategies for making money are radically different and the details of their strategies affect their success in the marketplace. Similarly, congregations need to look with great care at their strategies based upon their marketplace and spiritual gifts. What are their special talents? What opportunities will they bring to the market? How can they be good stewards of what they have? What does the marketplace call for?

Congregations have a wonderful opportunity to do strategic thinking every time they search for a new pastor. This point in the life of a congregation is the one certain, recurring event that can trigger serious rethinking. Of course, many congregations ignore the opportunity and look instead to continue whatever they were doing before. Even if they were doing well under the previous pastor, they may make the erroneous assumption that all they need to do is to continue the old system. Obviously, failure to review changes in context—such as their environment and their own resources—can be fatal. We will examine this in more detail in chapter 7.

The dilemma for Christians is that they are called to be *in* the world, not *of* the world. The typical mission statement usually tries to incorporate some of the tension: "We are called by God to minister in the world . . ." That suggests that we need to have some understanding of the world in which we live in order to have a coherent way of ministering in it.

A well-known simulation exercise, originating with the Canadian military, explores how survivors of a plane crash in a wilderness area in Canada might get back to civilization. The situation is that the plane has crashed; and they have a random assortment of items salvaged from the plane: some waterproof matches, a map, a bottle of rum, a canvas tarp, and so on. Corporate trainers using the exercise ask their trainees to figure out what to do in order to survive. One of the key elements in the exercise is knowledge about rescue operations in this kind of situation. With that knowledge, it becomes obvious that the survivors should not move from their location. Instead, they should put their energy into signaling the inevitable rescue plane. Attempting to walk out of the woods, given the resources they have, would be fatal for some or for all of the survivors. A group of trainees can get a fairly high score in the exercise without knowing about emergency rescue operations; however, for a high score that guarantees survival for all group members, the trainees must choose the correct strategy—that is, to stay put. So while the mission for every group encountering this exercise is survival, a high level of success depends on adopting strategies based on knowledge of the context—wilderness rescue procedures.

In the same way, the church mission statement is not enough to guarantee survival when a church is in the wilderness, no matter how passionate the church may be about it. There must be good strategic planning based on the mission statement, the available resources, and the reality of the context. *what is the context?*

The corporate world has moved away from traditional long-term planning. That planning model begins with a goal: in ten years this company will sell x units of product for a net income of y. In long-range planning the goal then determines the steps in reverse order. To be in a certain position in ten years we must be in this position in nine years, here in eight years, and so on. In a highly stable environment, that might be a fine way to plan. In our world today, with its enormous changes in technology, demography, and even climate every year, the context changes too rapidly. For the bakery/coffee shop, the mission is to make money by baking bread; the strategy is to combine product with the customers' expectation for service. The strategy is adequate because the bakery is sufficiently flexible to respond to changing customer needs.

A church needs to have a mission statement, but the church also needs to have a strategic plan based on sound strategic thinking. Good strategic thinking does not lock the church into trying to do the same "wonderful" thing year after year when there is no longer anyone who remembers or cares about doing that wonderful thing. Good strategic thinking frees up a church to think creatively, every day, about how it can best serve God in the world.

What to Do about It

Write a *mission statement* and refer to it frequently. One parish I visited had the congregation recite the mission statement in church every so often. Most mission statements for Christian churches will center on building up the Body of Christ or the kingdom of God, a serious task that requires some no-nonsense thinking and acting. Sometimes it means speaking the truth in love. Sometimes it means saying "no" to opportunities that just don't fit with the mission. This is not to say that ministry is not fun. On the contrary, if ministry isn't fun, the church members probably will not be passionate about it.

I have indicated that because the mission statement can be a trap if it is the only stated plan, it is also vital to have a *strategic plan* that proceeds naturally from the mission statement. Specific strategies can come from any of three sources:

1. Context—the real world in which the church exists (the neighborhood, the denomination, political and social factors, and so on)
2. Trajectory—the trends in the congregation that extend from the past to the future (more or less youth, more or less money, change of ethnicity, and so on)
3. Imagination—whatever the people may dream about doing in ministry

There is more information about each of these items in chapter 6.

Once assembled, a strategic plan is not a locked-in path like a big red line on a map; it is a set of core values and goals that can be a compass in the wilderness. When a church is faced with making decisions, the strategic plan can point the way even if it does not show all of the bends in the road.

5 Decisions

Some churches have little idea what they want or need for good decision-making processes.

So they proposed two, Joseph . . . and Matthias. Then they prayed and said, "Lord, you know everyone's heart. Show us which one of these two you have chosen to take the place in this ministry and apostleship from which Judas turned aside to go to his own place." And they cast lots for them, and the lot fell on Matthias; and he was added to the eleven apostles.
–Acts 1:23–26

In our highly rational era, we may think it quaint or odd to make decisions by casting lots—even the prayerful casting of lots. However, there was more at work here than a roll of the dice or the intervention of the Holy Spirit. Since the apostles took time and care to select only two possible men, they must have already established priorities based on some criteria they had identified.

We would like to think that we make decisions in an orderly way with the right amount of guidance from the Holy Spirit. Even so, many churches make decisions in a haphazard way that might as well be a random casting of lots. All too often committees and councils arrive at decisions without considering all of the possibilities or all of the consequences.

What Is the Decision and Who Will Make It?

Suppose that the buildings and grounds committee receives complaints from the choir that every time it rains they get wet while sitting in the choir stalls. One might reasonably conclude that the roof needs to be fixed. That may be the best solution, but it is not the only solution. What exactly is the problem? The stated problem was that the choir does not like to get wet during Sunday worship. Two inexpensive solutions would be either to issue umbrellas to the choir or to have them sit elsewhere. While these may be silly ideas, either one solves the stated problem. If good research reveals that there is a leak in the roof, one might conclude that the roof should be repaired. Unfortunately, the roof may be so old that it needs to be replaced. Furthermore, there may be so much water damage that other parts of the building need to be repaired or replaced. The choir's complaint could lead to a capital fund drive for a major remodeling or reconstruction job. Alternatively, the council could issue umbrellas. Clarity in decision making first requires knowing what the problem is and then moving through all of the possibilities.

Lack of clarity about the decision to be made, who is entitled to make the decision, and how that person or persons are to go about making the decision can all lead a church to do dumb things. It does not matter so much what the preferred process is in a particular church—voting, consensus, or executive order; nor does it matter especially which person or persons are empowered to make the decision—pastor, committee, council, or whole congregation. What matters is having an agreed-upon decision-making process that is appropriate to the congregation and the situation.

Votes and consensus, teams and hierarchies, casting lots and detailed research—all are valid components for decision making in the church. For structure, some churches have a slew of committees while others have only a single council composed of individuals who handle particular tasks. For leadership style, some congregations prefer a strong leader who goes boldly into the future while others are content to drift. Authority can reside in any of one or more places: the pastor, the board or vestry, or the congregation itself. Every church has a decision-making process that is some mixture of these components, which may be clear or ambiguous. The resulting management style is further shaped by a variety of factors, such as denominational polity, local polity, tradition, the previous bad experience, the previous positive experience, and the culture in which the church resides, to name just a few. Sometimes these elements are incompatible with each other or are simply not understood. If that is the case, the congregation will have a difficult time making decisions in a way that will lead them where God is or may be pointing them.The dumb thing that churches do is to fail to know or understand both their actual management style and their preferences for management style.

I would like to describe three factors that frame the management style of congregations, any one of which can cause a serious problem.

The dumb thing that churches do is to fail to know or understand both their actual management style and their preferences for management style.

Church Size

Arlin Rothauge's monograph *Sizing Up a Congregation for New Member Ministry*[6] has defined some of the dynamics of congregations based on their size. The "family," "pastoral," "program," and "corporate" churches all have different management needs and expectations. Pastors who ignore these needs and expectations do so at their peril. Boards and search committees who do not understand these needs and expectations navigate their churches purely by dumb luck. People involved in church management as volunteers or professionals should have at least a passing knowledge of the types of congregations based on size and how that knowledge applies to their own congregation. I particularly recommend Roy Oswald's essay[7] on the role of the pastor in these various congregations; it is summarized below.

The Family Church

This congregation with an average Sunday attendance of not more than fifty people really operates like a chapel on a wealthy landowner's estate. One or two families will hold the power in this congregation. The pastor is not expected to lead, but rather to minister to the people in the parish. Any plans regarding the church building or program must be cleared with the leading family. The pastor who does not follow this ancient prescription will be eased out the door fairly quickly.

The Pastoral Church

Fifty to one hundred fifty people attend this church every Sunday. The congregation is still small enough that the pastor will personally know all of the members of the congregation. The pastor will be expected to lead this congregation spiritually through preaching and visitation and to meet with lay leadership to make the congregation function. This church is large enough to need the pastor to be the leader, but small enough for each member to assume personal input to the decision-making process by virtue of his or her personal relationship with the pastor.

The Program Church

The program church is large enough that the pastor realistically can no longer have a personal relationship with all of the members, as there are 150 to 350 people attending on Sunday. Either a second ordained person is part of the staff or some system of lay help must exist to provide a personal connection to the administration. In either case, the pastor now presides over a multiple staff with lines of communication that connect the members and the staff as well as clusters or interest groups. Some of the members are directly involved in the decision-making process by holding positions on committees and councils, but most of the people are one or more steps removed from decisions in the church. Many congregations have had enormous trouble making the transition from pastoral to program size or from program to pastoral size because the requisite management styles are so radically different in these two types of churches. The problem with transition from the pastoral to the program church is that as a church grows, the members continue to expect that they will each have a personal relationship with the pastor well past the point that this is possible. Going the other way, as a church shrinks from program to pastoral size, the leaders may hold onto staff or programs when a sufficient number of people no longer exists to justify them. Either situation is highly frustrating for all concerned.

The Corporate Church

With more than 350 in attendance on Sunday, this congregation must be deliberate about finding ways to organize into smaller groups around particular interests or particular members of the staff. While this is in many ways just a larger version of the program church, the pastor of the corporate church assumes a role that requires that he or she work more with staff than with members. If he or she was hired because of great preaching skills, then one can expect that the senior pastor will spend a great deal of time writing sermons while the staff handles most pastoral calls and the routine work of the parish. Perhaps this senior pastor is the kind who likes to micromanage, but unless he or she is particularly brilliant at this, the senior pastor will have no time for any hospital visits or quality sermon preparation. Decisions in the corporate-sized parish must move along clear paths or be lost altogether. The members who want to be involved in the decision making of this church will need to be aggressive in seeking the right persons or committees to state their case or join in the process themselves.

It is not too hard to see where problems arise. A congregation may be of one size, have expectations for another size, hire a pastor with skills for yet another size, and no one, including the new pastor, may know the difference.

For example, it once was common practice for judicatory leaders to send newly minted clergy fresh from seminary directly into little family-sized congregations. How much harm could they cause? The young pastor would show up with a notebook full of ideas and crash and burn in months: "These people don't want to do anything, change anything, or learn anything." The seminary did not tell the neophytes about the special dynamics of the small church. There may have been no one on the faculty who ever pastored a small church. On the other hand, the small churches who received these inexperienced clergy sensed the education gap and saw their role as being a training ground. They would be polite, but they would continue to run the church their way, "training" one neophyte after another.

A variation on this dynamic is the larger church that is actually run by a "few good men," usually three to five lay people— probably professional types—who, along with their fathers before them, have run the church for years. They may take turns being on the council, session, or vestry. They may actually include the male pastor as "one of the guys." Fortunately, this leadership model, which has been around for a long time, is breaking up as women enter the ministry.

Pastor's Style, Congregation's Style

Since in all congregations the pastor plays some sort of role of in the decision-making processes of the church, the pastor's own gifts and preferences for management style are important. Some pastors, for example, prefer to work alone as opposed to working with others; they go into the office, read Scripture, pray, study a problem, and announce a course of action. Others may do all of those things but also talk it over with the board or certain key lay people and keep refining the solution until a solid proposal is ready. Some pastors will then try out the solution on others in the congregation before implementing a new concept or program. There is no right or wrong here. Either management style will work, depending upon the problem to be solved and the context.

A second polarity has at one end the pastor who is more passive and reactive as opposed to the pastor who is active or even proactive. The former prefers to respond to events in and around the congregation, providing hands-on pastoral help. The latter is more likely to preach prophetic sermons and press for innovation. Again, both can be good management styles depending upon the circumstances.

If we put these two polarities together, we have the following grid:

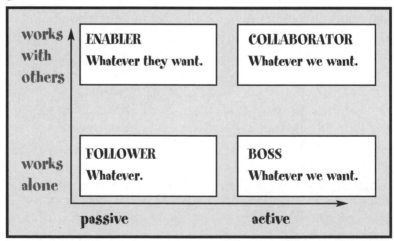

works with others ↑	**ENABLER** Whatever they want.	**COLLABORATOR** Whatever we want.
works alone	**FOLLOWER** Whatever.	**BOSS** Whatever we want.
	passive	active →

A pastor who is a Boss would be miserable in a family-sized parish. The Enabler and Follower will frustrate the corporate or program church; however, even these generalizations are risky. There may come a time in the life of a corporate church when the members are learning to assert themselves and a pastor who is an Enabler is what they need. On the other hand, a family church may need a kick in the pants from a Boss.

Unfortunately, many clergy do not know what their management style is, since they never stop working long enough to find out. Furthermore, most congregations might be able to articulate the management qualities they want in a pastor, but too often, these are expressed in terms of the previous pastor. "We want a pastor who is more organized than Fred was." "We want a pastor who won't try to tell the board what to do the way Susan did." Seminaries do not teach very much management, nor do they necessarily help their students determine what their personal management style might be. Likewise, a congregation may or may not have ever gone through the effort required to learn what their preferred management style is—they just keep doing things the same way. The problem, again, is a lack of self-awareness.

One not entirely self-aware corporate-sized congregation assigned memorial gifts of flowers for the altar by first considering who gave what and when the previous year. The Goodbody family always gave the flowers for Palm Sunday and had been doing so for twenty years. Another family, the Newcomers, wanted to memorialize Grandma Newcomer who died recently by giving the flowers on the Sunday nearest her birthday, which happened to be at the end of March and which also happened to be Palm Sunday. The collision of the two families was troublesome because both families refused to budge. The staff and the council of this generally well-organized church, accustomed to clearly defined, collaborative decisions, spent many hours hammering out a compromise for the immediate conflict and then constructing a coherent general policy. The church leaders discovered from this exercise that they had a number of similar procedures that fit under the heading of "We always did it this way," although the old way was no longer appropriate. Consequently, the staff and lay leaders began to look for outdated processes and fix them.

One management style that, God willing, is dying off, is the pastor who does everything. This person may or may not be a workaholic, but he (usually he) makes all the decisions. This autocratic leader is in the lower right quadrant of the grid. While this pastor may be a benign dictator, he is a tough act to follow. Churches who have had one such pastor for twenty or more years have such a weak concept of lay leadership that they have trouble even conducting a coherent search for a new pastor.

Polity

Sometimes polity—the rules and practices of a denomination—helps or confuses decision-making processes. In the Episcopal Church, canon law states that rectors are responsible for the spiritual life of a ministry and the vestry is responsible for the physical and financial life of a ministry. One can make a good case for all things temporal having some spiritual connection or value. Similarly, one can make a good case for the importance of lay leadership in all aspects of ministry. So while the denominational rules spell out a division of authority, they do not spell out the actual borders of the two areas of authority. For example, is the furniture in the sanctuary (the altar, the choir stalls, and so on) under the authority of the rector or of the vestry? This becomes a serious issue if one or the other wants to move or otherwise change any of the furniture. Most church members do not discover the details of their denomination's rules until there is a conflict. Sorting through the conflict at times like these—without knowing the rules—is like trying to play baseball without knowing how a runner can safely reach base.

A more congregational polity, such as that of the United Church of Christ, American Baptists, Southern Baptists, Disciples of Christ, and others, presents another set of problems. If power in the parish is ultimately vested in the congregation, how do the pastor and other staff members make daily decisions? Every congregation must work through this problem in their own way. Committees, councils, deacons, boards, and staff must somehow create a harmonious system with a high degree of trust. As always, the pastor is at the center, but that does not mean that the pastor has any real authority. One such congregation has an extremely elaborate committee system that ultimately feeds into a church council. Consensus is the preferred method for making decisions within these bodies, so it often takes a long time to make even simple decisions. The twelve-person staff is regarded as simply one piece in a large puzzle, with no more weight than any one of the committees. Such a system may seem quaint and naïve to some or bold and "cutting edge" to others. This congregation is not unhappy or in turmoil. In fact, a key part of their self-understanding is that they want to be as inclusive as possible in all aspects of their ministry—including decision making. I have found churches like this in all branches of the faith, even in the more hierarchical Episcopal Church. For these kinds of congregations, I suspect that ministry is at least partially in the *process* of decision making as much as in the result. Their motto might be that of the passenger steamship line of another era: "Getting there is half the fun." Difficulty arises only when there is conflict or some issue that needs to be decided quickly. Then the system becomes awkward as authority spreads outward over the congregation and responsibility heads inward to the staff.

Churches need not copy the decision-making systems of businesses in order to gain clarity because a fundamental difference in the self-understanding of most businesses and all churches is in their concept of ultimate authority. While churches do need to be able to state clearly how they make decisions, they also need to remember who the ultimate "Boss" is. While the earliest church may look naïve to us for making a personnel decision by drawing lots, I admire the faith of a community that so relies on God.

What to Do about It
- Be certain that the person or persons with the responsibility for making a decision have the authority to do so.
- Try following this process for making a decision:
    1. Know what the decision is (review the example about the choir being rained on in this chapter).
    2. Freely brainstorm all of the possibilities without evaluation.
    3. Check again to be certain that the decision to be made is clear.
    4. Evaluate thoroughly all of the possible solutions (don't forget to include cost estimates, if applicable).
    5. Select the best choice.
    6. Establish the next steps (who will do what and when).
    7. Build in a procedure for evaluation.

6 Identity

Sometimes churches do not know who they are or to what ministry God is calling them.

Examine yourselves to see whether you are living in the faith.
Test yourselves. Do you not realize that Jesus Christ is in
you?—unless, indeed, you fail to meet the test!
–2 Corinthians 13:5

There is hardly a religious philosophy or self-help program that doesn't teach the importance of self-knowledge. We learn who we are through reflection on our experiences and through the observations of others. This is sometimes a painful process, so we may be reluctant to enter into it either as individuals or churches.

Congregations weave the tapestries of their identities over a period of years with threads consisting of the strengths and weaknesses of the leaders, pledging patterns, responses to local social issues, and other strands both bright and subtle. I grew up in a church that prided itself on several things: urban ministry (including a free medical clinic), great preaching, and a Christmas pageant of epic proportions. When I was seven, the congregation moved into a new, modern church built where the old neo-Gothic church had stood. The old parish hall, also neo-Gothic, was retained. For years afterwards, the church's logo included reference to the new building by means of some portion of its distinctive silhouette. Surprisingly, as I write this chapter, on my desk is a recent publication from my former church that features the neo-Gothic tower of the old parish building. The logo is in a Gothic script. What this new imaging conveys is a sense of traditional Episcopal/Anglican values, not the "church-in-the-city" values of a previous generation. Is this a real change for the congregation?

Or was the real identity always conservative and traditional—and we kidded ourselves about the urban ministry image? Or are they both genuine?

In a corporate-sized church (350 or more worshipers on an average Sunday), there can be many self-images in circulation, all of them valid. Furthermore, it is reasonable to suppose that any church's identity may change over time. The problem is not with the multiple but valid self-descriptions a church may have; the problem is the accuracy of the self-concept. Illusion about oneself—for an individual or for a congregation—can lead to the problems described in this book.

When is a good time to investigate identity? Any time. Most congregations are sufficiently fluid with members coming and going that all one can hope for is a snapshot of a particular identity. As soon as the picture is taken, it is almost immediately outdated. Only a series of snapshots gives the identity a sense of direction. Are young families moving into the neighborhood? Is there a change in the ethnic makeup of the congregation? There

---

The dumb thing that churches do is to analyze their identities incorrectly or not at all.

---

are some opportunities that arise that inevitably trigger self-analysis: a change of pastor, a major conflict, a large monetary gift, a catastrophic fire, or a major building program. Any of these events should cause the congregation to do some self-examination or risk a major error in whatever they do next.

But there is no need to wait for circumstances to overtake you. Proactively investigating who you are and what God is calling you to do is always worth the effort. The dumb thing that churches do is to analyze their identities incorrectly or not at all. The congregation that inaccurately thinks of itself as weak in resources will not use its endowment creatively. The church that thinks of itself as a pastoral-sized church when it is solidly in the range of a program-sized church will expect its pastor to visit everyone regularly, even if it is impossible. The pastor who mistakes a family church for a pastoral church will constantly fail as a leader because the church already has one in the form of a patriarch/matriarch. The congregation that likes their administrator-pastor but secretly yearns for a spiritual leader will always feel less than whole.

To assess its identity accurately, a church needs to look at a number of components. While there are many threads in the tapestry of identity, I will group them into six areas that are especially important to a congregation.

The People

A congregation is as strong as the community of volunteers who do the work of ministry. Paul's letters make it clear that at the heart of the church there are people with a variety of spiritual gifts and that the church needs all of those gifts to continue building up the Body of Christ. It is not part of our faith to reject any one gift in favor of another. You take what you have and, with the help of the Holy Spirit, make something of it, both individually and corporately. So the first question for any church is: What do you have?

People have gifts of all sorts ranging from technical skills that are applied in a vocation such as nursing or welding to artistic talents that produce music and pottery. All of these are needed in the Body of Christ. There are talents for parenting, teaching, and persuading that have obvious uses in the church; there are also some important gifts that are hidden. For example, many retired people have the gift of time. The fact that they are available during the day means they can do some things in the church that most of the working adult members cannot.

The difficulty lies in discerning the gifts that are available in a particular congregation. This goes beyond the administrative headache of keeping a talent database up-to-date. There is also the matter of persuading people to reveal or offer a talent. I was several years in a ministry before I discovered that a member of the congregation was an outstanding harpist. She had simply put this talent on hold while pursuing other interests, but was delighted when asked to offer her gift in the service of the church. People with professional skills may be reluctant to offer those skills in their off hours. A CPA who crunches numbers all day may not want to be the treasurer and crunch the church's numbers in the evening. Gifts discernment workshops for churches of all kinds are often available through your own judicatory, the local council of churches, or pastors' groups.

The inverse of persuading people to offer their gifts in the service of the church is discouraging people from volunteering for jobs for which they are not suited. To use Paul's analogy of the Body of Christ as an actual body, it won't work to try to convert a hand into a nose. Even if your CPA member is unwilling to become the treasurer, that fact should not be an invitation to the checkbook-challenged to take the position.

Each individual also brings his or her own personality into the congregation. In several churches where I have worked, the congregation was blessed by having in their midst a highly extroverted person who was the self-appointed greeter. One such grandmotherly woman went up to every new face she saw on a Sunday morning and struck up a conversation. She was able to remember the little details about the newcomer's family or vocation and use those facts when seeing the same person the next week. Many members of the church traced their decision to join the congregation to this woman. She was a valuable and beloved part of her parish. Similarly, I have nearly always had an introvert in the congregation who could maintain his or her own spiritual life as well as contemplate the collective spiritual life of the congregation. Such a person provides a point of stability by modeling a way of sorting out and prioritizing issues in the life of the congregation.

Furthermore, people are individuals with their own dreams and needs—these are a part of the congregation as well. One person might have been recently diagnosed with cancer, while another has found and joined a support group for cancer patients. One may want to explore spirituality through painting, while another is a painter seeking a teaching opportunity. It is challenging to envision a parish survey that captures all of this information. The data we would have about our parishioners would emerge as a list of needs and dreams as well as talents. However, no matter how sophisticated the database may be, the actual connecting of one person with another happens one person at a time. The pastor or pastoral team and the internal networks of the parish especially make these connections during social occasions such as the Sunday morning coffee hour and chats before committee meetings. This is one reason why these events are so vital to the life of the church. They afford opportunities for the community to minister to itself. A congregation that does not have a chance to make these connections is a Body of Christ with a faulty nervous system: it does not connect to itself.

When all of these people actually come together and interact, they become an organic group—the Body of Christ. They develop a collective identity. How do we define the shape and substance of the body as a whole? At the most basic level there are demographic data to consider: How old are the members? What family configurations do they have? What is their ethnic background? What is their level of education? Where are they employed? How much do they earn? Where do they stand politically? Do their children go to public or private schools? And so on.

Right now, many churches are concerned about the rising average age of their congregations. Sometimes churches wonder why they do not have a successful youth group, even though the average age of the congregation is such that their children have grown up and are forming families of their own somewhere else. Having accurate statistics improves strategic planning for this kind of church. Congregations can then choose either to initiate intensive recruiting to draw in families with children or to concentrate on ministry to and with the existing population. It is a waste of precious resources to fund an unnecessary ministry; accurate self-knowledge can prevent this kind of waste.

History
Another thread of identity is the collective memory that is tied to the heart and soul of a congregation. What do people think of when they are asked about the history of their church? Is the history about conflicts, about constructing buildings, about sponsoring new churches, or something else? Are church members likely to list the wonderful pastors they have had or just the courageous founding pastor? Does this church pride itself on its advocacy of civil rights, women's rights, or gay rights? Is there an apocryphal story people like to tell about their church? Does the congregation still have some shame around the pastor who committed suicide or the treasurer who embezzled church funds? Memories may be positive or negative, accurate or inaccurate. Just about every church has some wounds in its history; while time may heal all wounds, time does not remove the scars. Both the positive and negative elements of its history are important in the psyche of a church.

It may not be a dumb thing, but it is certainly a sad thing when a church's identity is totally bound up in its history. I worked with one such church that had been a strong and vibrant congregation in the 1930s through the 1950s and had assembled a substantial endowment. Their town had been an important rail center and many famous people had spent a night or two in the grand old hotel near the station. Gradually, the railroad declined and local industries moved elsewhere. The change was slow; over a period of fifty years, people left this congregation by aging and death or by retiring and moving elsewhere. When I came across this congregation, there was little or no present ministry and virtually no hope for a future ministry. They clung to an identity that consisted of their glorious past history, symbolically represented by their Tiffany stained glass windows. They viewed their endowment as a resource to keep the building in good condition (commensurate with its status as a historical site), and had great difficulty seeing the possibilities for a new ministry funded by the endowment. The history of the parish was the bulk of their identity, and it was killing them.

The history is an important part of the present and future life of a church, but it is only one of several parts. The church that calcifies around its history, whether glorious or infamous, does not have a future. Unless your history is also "America's History" is currently supported

Culture

The next four threads are subtler than the list of talents and the history of a congregation. For that reason, they are more likely to be troublesome. The culture of the institution is the first of these threads.

These days, cultural climate in the workplace is a hot topic. There is a significant difference between working for Procter and Gamble and working for a start-up software company. One is a huge organization with divisions and a range of job levels, while the other may be a team of ten people with more or less equal responsibility.

But what is the cultural climate of a congregation? It is not easy to identify, especially if you are looking at the congregation from the inside. However, the history and context of a church shape the cultural climate, and those elements are readily accessible. In about half the congregations in which I have worked, I learned early in my tenure that the congregation was not interested in literary references in my sermons. The problem was not that they were uneducated, it was simply that their interests lay elsewhere than in reading books. They appreciated sermon illustrations that were immediate and factual. The engineering students in my current campus ministry are the same way. Understanding the character and culture of a church's identity is very important for the pastor.

Another cultural factor is that of the denomination. The denomination has a theology, rules and procedures, and its own identity that the congregation may choose to emphasize or hide. The denomination may also be wrestling with its own questions: the role of women in the church, the role of gays and lesbians in the church, the authority of church leaders, ecumenical relations, and church growth. A particular congregation may choose to take an aggressive stand on one side or another of these issues and so shape its own identity.

Context

The context of a congregation is not necessarily hard to see, but since we see our context every day, we forget that it is there and that it impacts our churches. Simply put, the church does not exist in a vacuum. The building is located in a neighborhood and that neighborhood is probably changing. The neighborhood is in a community that may be urban or rural, suburban or ex-urban. A single employer such as a corporate headquarters or a university may dominate the community. The geography might make the context a resort or a mining town, with attendant pros and cons.

The political context of the city, county, state, and country in which the congregation resides may raise issues such as capital punishment, lotteries and legalized gambling, international relations and conflicts, or environmental concerns. A congregation may have a tendency to take united stands in political debates, may be torn apart by them, or may simply ignore them.

Rules, Policies, and Norms

Possibly the most easily overlooked pieces of a church's identity are its accumulated rules, policies, and norms. The rules of a congregation may include the articles of incorporation, charter, or bylaws. Rules define distinctions between congregations, especially those of different denominations. The rules invariably define authority in the church—who is in charge and who makes what decisions. For example, in a congregational church there are usually some precise rules about how to call a meeting of the congregation, who presides at such a meeting, and what kinds of decisions the congregation can make. Every church has important rules about how a pastor is called and dismissed and how money is handled, among other topics. Much of a church's rules-based identity can be summed up with the word *polity*, which is the way that the church goes about its most important decisions at the local, regional, or national level. The most critical element of any polity is who is in charge: the congregation, the pastor, the bishop, the association, the synod, the convention, or the Pope.

Policies are the stated procedures and preferences of the church and are less formal than rules; for example, the treasurer chairs the finance committee, the staff report to the pastor, or the board meets every second Tuesday. Policies cover any topic from salaries and benefits to decision-making procedures. Rules and policies differ in how they are formed. Making rules usually requires some official procedure that is itself bounded by rules, such as the annual meeting of the church, judicatory, or denomination. Policy, on the other hand, may be simply the *stated* preferences of the church leaders. The identity of a church is shaped by its policies to the extent that they set a tone for how the church conducts its business. Is the church highly structured or loosely structured? Are there multiple hoops of administrative procedure to jump through or is decision making streamlined? One church with which I was associated had a policy that all clergy on staff had to wear black shoes while on the premises. That policy defined the tone for that church.

Norms, while similar to policies, may be sufficiently below the surface that few can articulate them. Norms are prevailing tacit assumptions about the life of the congregation that may reach back into the history. These threads are the subtlest of all; when identified, they often prompt the statement, "We've always done it this way."

- The pastor always parks in a certain place.
- Mrs. Goodbody always sits in a certain pew.
- One family always gives the flowers for the Christmas Eve service.

- The authority of the pastor is always suspect (or never suspect).
- We begin each meeting with prayer.
- Even when our council meetings are stressful, we don't insult each other.
- We dress up when we come to worship.

Some tacit assumptions are quite dangerous and need to be exposed, while others are benign and can safely be exercised for years. For example, one Episcopal church took as a norm that the vestry, in consultation with the congregation, made all decisions. They were unaware that it was a rule of the Episcopal Church that the rector was responsible for decisions regarding worship, that the vestry was responsible for the physical property, that the congregation only voted to elect the vestry, and that the bishop of the diocese was the ultimate authority. Getting clear about the rules and norms was a major step in recovering serenity in this church. New norms can develop every time something is done the same way twice, so every church must be diligent in testing its assumptions. Every time someone says, "We always did it this way," a loud siren should go off throughout the church building.

Deeply embedded norms are sometimes difficult to bring into the light; they are always difficult to change. Several times I have seen congregations that consisted of sensible folk, mostly professional and middle management types. They were wonderful individuals, warm and generous. However, when they came together in the church for a committee or council meeting, some other collective identity took hold of them that was grasping and vindictive. I suspect that they could not let go of certain disappointments in their church history. They routinely denied that there were any problems of their own making while they continued to play out old, self-destructive patterns. As a result, any meeting of any group could turn ugly fairly quickly. Their norms included concepts of ministry and decision making that gave emphasis to emotion, feelings, and undocumented assumptions.

Calling

Where a congregation is headed as an organization is also part of the fabric of identity. "A response to a calling" should describe a prayerfully considered decision to engage in an activity that is believed to be in line with God's will. A church that knows who it is but has no idea what God is calling it to do is a church that is standing still, wandering, or possibly running full tilt toward a cliff. It does not matter if the church is large or small; discernment of the calling should precede the strategic planning. A calling should precede the search for a new pastor, major construction, or a missionary project. Not all callings need to lead boldly into the future. Churches that are highly stressed financially may legitimately feel for a period of time that their calling is simply to survive. It is even possible that a church may feel called to die. That is not unreasonable; there is no rule that says that institutions must live indefinitely. Members of a congregation may feel their particular church body is called to die so that something else can have new life. The ultimate model for this decision is the death and resurrection of Jesus Christ.

The tapestry of a church's identity may have some worn spots, stains, historic pieces, visionary lines, multiple colors, or shades of gray; and furthermore, there are changes occurring every day. Having a grasp of the church's identity and tying it to God's call will inevitably bring about powerful ministry. The key is to name and claim the whole tapestry.

What to Do about It

Take the time to learn the identity of the congregation:

- The available resources of time, talent, and treasure.
- The decision-making processes.
- Theology—at least the practical theology that backs up the congregation's assumptions about who it is.
- Sense of calling, vision, mission statement, strategic plan.
- Rules, policies, and norms for the denomination and the congregation.
- Key points in the history of the church.

For this last item, construct a timeline. You may know the procedure: place a length of butcher paper on a wall where everyone in the congregation can have access to it. The length of the paper is determined by how much history you need to write on it. At the left end place the date of the founding of the church and at the right end the current date. Have the church historian place a few key items on the timeline—the dates of the pastorates, the year the parish hall burned down, and so on. Then let everyone in the congregation write on it whatever they remember: the time the new minister spilled a full pitcher of communion wine all over the altar, the year the new organ was built, the year the congregation met in a trailer, and so on. Then everyone will have an opportunity to see what their fellow parishioners think is important about the church's history.

Make all of the information about the church's identity available to the members as well as to newcomers and use this information in designing ministry. Work on the hidden norms ("We always did it this way.") in the congregation and expose them to the light of day. Then either discard them or make them visible policy.

7 Pastoral Transition

Some churches mishandle the time between pastorates.

It is the LORD who goes before you. He will be with you; he will not fail you or forsake you. Do not fear or be dismayed. (Moses, speaking to Joshua, is describing the transition of leadership.)
–Deuteronomy 31:8

M y wife and I hate moving. Having done a lot of moving in our lives, including moving from one side of the country to the other and back, we would like to stay in the city, neighborhood, and house we are in right now. (I have a suspicion that just putting this thought into print is a sure way to signal God that we should be called to move.) There are some nomads who prefer to be always on the move, but most of us like to have a few things settled—a few things that we can count on—especially our churches. A body can handle only so much change.

Several of the other nine dumb things that churches do are simply bad responses to the inevitability of change. But God has not made a static universe, so we had best figure out how to deal with changes in the world.

The Anxiety of Pastoral Transition

The most pervasive and certain element of change for a congregation is that from one pastor to another. Predictably, most congregations do not like this change unless they do not like the departing pastor. Most of the time when a pastor resigns and goes to another ministry, the congregation feels abandoned, like a child missing a departed parent, just as many of us did as we tearfully watched Mom or Dad drive away from our school for the first time. Children may experience a sudden rush of terror, scream, and cry. Likewise, many congregations can behave like young children or adolescents when the pastor leaves.

Sometimes church members cannot wait for their pastor to leave. In one case, a pastor had initiated an amazing amount of new ministry in the congregation, but some members began trying to undo it as soon as he announced that he was leaving. Those who were thrilled by the pastor's creative approach to ministry were deeply distressed by the efforts of those who tried to undo it. When the pastor actually left, some parishioners felt relieved to see him go, while others felt abandoned. When abandonment is the dominant feeling in the congregation, the church board will be under pressure to get a new pastor as soon as possible. If the board responds to the impulse to fill the vacancy as soon as possible, they are likely to miss one of the most important opportunities in ministry.

Transition is scary. I remember a story about a trapeze artist who described what it was like to go tumbling through the air from his trapeze to the "catcher" on another trapeze. He said that the hardest part was not the complex timing involved in making the transition from trapeze to air to catcher. The hardest part for him was letting go of his trapeze in the first place. As soon as he was tumbling in space, he was too busy to be nervous or afraid. The church that takes its transition seriously will be so busy during the transition that it will not have time to be afraid.

Ministry in the Transition

What will the church be doing during the transition? Three things. First, if their polity allows for a significant time for transition with an interim pastor, they will do some work closing out the previous pastorate. Whether that pastorate was a positive or negative experience, there is always some grief or even trauma around the departure as well as a ministry to celebrate and commemorate. Everything from an exit interview with the outgoing pastor to a retirement party is in order. Second, the ministry of the church needs to go on as before. People do not stop giving birth, having emergencies, or dying just because the beloved pastor retired or left; the interim pastor, lay ministers, board, and other leaders need to attend to the ongoing spiritual life of the congregation. Third, the church needs to invest some time and energy in taking a good look at its identity and calling as outlined in the previous chapter.

Four Keys to a Successful Pastoral Search

I stated previously that a church in transition between pastorates has a special opportunity to reflect on its identity and calling. We can expand on that idea, beginning with this brief summary of four keys to the pastoral search process:

1. The congregation should know who they are.
2. The congregation should know where God is calling them.
3. The pastoral candidate should know who he or she is.
4. The pastoral candidate should know where God is calling him or her.

While these four points may seem simple, it is the rare congregation and the rare new pastor who have done all four things well. Too many churches do not take the time to assess properly who they are and where they are headed at any time, including during a search. Too many clergy delude themselves about their skills and their calling. Saint Paul says, "There are many gifts and one Spirit." One of the implications of this statement is that it is unnecessary for any one person—including clergy—to have all of the gifts. (In fact, the essence of Paul's message is that the diversity of gifts of the Spirit is a wonderful part of the fabric of creation.) The task, then, for clergy and laity, is to discern what gifts they have and how best to use them in their particular manifestation of the Body of Christ. This requires a search committee to do its homework and learn all they can about the identity of their congregation and its calling. (See chapter 6 for more details on this process.) Then they must discern, as best they are able, the gifts and calling of the candidates for the pastorate. Likewise, pastors must do their homework and their own prayerful discerning.

Failing to Use the Four Keys

The results of a church's failing to assess itself properly can be seen in the case of St. Swithin's-in-the-Suburb, which went through the search process without any serious investigation of its history or of trends in the church or neighborhood. The congregation was founded in the 1950s on the edge of Our City in the midst of a new housing project in a comfortable, middle class neighborhood, home to many employees of a nearby corporation that was expanding rapidly. The large company liked to rotate its young engineers and executives through a variety of work settings and this town was one rung on the corporate ladder. Consequently, the neighborhood in which the church was placed was the home for young professionals with families. These families typically bought a house with a mortgage, had another child or two, stayed for three to five years, and moved on. The church profile consisted of many energetic and optimistic young couples with children. The church in this context was imbued with its own aura of upward mobility.

The church property was developed in several stages with money from the denomination in the form of low-interest loans. The leaders of the church made the same reasonable assumptions about the future of the church that they made in their own lives: the church would always be able to pay the mortgage because the economic base would always be there.

Nonetheless, changes in technology and in the marketplace forced the large company to alter some of its strategies. Fewer young executives were rotated through the local plants and offices. Some got stuck in Our City or were given no chance of advancement and bailed out. The neighborhood around the church began to change. The average age of homeowners rose. The value of real estate was flat or dropping. Other businesses began to have trouble because of the economic disappearing act of the large company.

At the church, everyone continued to believe that they were growing. They looked at the ever-increasing budget and assumed that the rising pledge total meant that they were continuing to be successful. They routinely put "new pledges" on the income side of their budget but neglected to list "lost pledges" on the expense side. During this period, their pastor of fifteen years resigned and went to a church in another part of the country. A search committee was formed that subsequently offered data in the church's profile showing a high degree of economic success for the congregation. The reality was that attendance was slowly dropping, as were pledge units. The only rising number was the average pledge. St. Swithin's still looked like a growing, or at least stable, institution.

St. Swithin's leaders continued to assume that the world was a benign place where upward mobility was the norm in spite of ample evidence to the contrary. The fact that this congregation failed to understand the profound changes in their context caused them to make a number of serious errors. The congregation made an assumption about their long-term financial context. Unfortunately, that context changed almost overnight and without notice. The search committee did not spot this change and, consequently, drew up an inaccurate profile. The inaccurate profile led to calling the wrong pastor with the wrong management style and the wrong cultural background. For that and other reasons, St. Swithin's was in turmoil for several years.

Unfortunately, this story is not uncommon. All too often, search committees fail to spend enough time and energy building a profile that truly articulates the identity of their church.

Problems with Search Committees

Unintended Ignorance

One reason for failing to do the homework properly is a failure to understand the assignment. Many search committees do not immediately grasp the special nature of the relationship of a pastor to a church. When people who do hiring in their professional lives dominate the search committee, these well-intentioned folk may force on the entire committee the assumption that the search for a new pastor is not unlike hiring upper management for a corporation. They will claim, correctly, that there are certain skills and levels of experience essential for the job. They appropriately define a certain level of education and maturity necessary for the position. While all of these factors are important in the search for a pastor, there is one element that is unique to a church. The relationship of a pastor to a congregation is more akin to that of a marriage relationship than employer-employee. The connection between the pastor and the people needs to reside at a deep level— soul to soul. The responsibility of the search committee is to connect one soul to a group of souls, and that task goes well beyond consideration of job skills. Consequently, members of a search committee must reveal to each other their deepest thoughts and feelings about their faith and their church. The task requires a high level of cohesion in the small group that in turn requires a high degree of trust. Unless the convener of the group is very experienced in both group process and the mechanics of the pastoral search process, the likelihood of failure is high.

Because the task of calling a pastor does not come up very often in the life of a congregation, most search committees consist mostly or entirely of people who have never been on a search committee before. If left to their own devices, they may or may not produce a coherent parish profile and may or may not have any clear idea of what kind of pastoral leadership the congregation needs.

Another common issue is the "forest and trees" phenomenon. It is very difficult to be entirely objective in the process of producing one's own parish profile—a profile that will be accurate and make sense to someone with no knowledge of the congregation, its traditions, current and previous difficulties, and local conditions. For the necessary experience and objectivity, I think it is important for pastoral search committees to engage the services of an outsider—either the appropriate staff person from the judicatory office or a consultant who specializes in this kind of work. Again, I want to draw a comparison with marriage. Most clergy spend a substantial amount of time with a couple before performing their wedding ceremony. Because clergy conduct many weddings and most people get married only once, or possibly twice, the experience of the pastor can be very helpful. There are some common pitfalls to look for as the couple describes their relationship, reasons for getting married, and understanding of the vows. The wise pastor can spare a couple a lot of grief by pointing out weaknesses that need attention in the relationship. Similarly, there are a number of common pitfalls for search committees that the judicatory staff person or search consultant can help the committee avoid.

Whitewashing

One such pitfall is leaving out of the church's history in the profile any mention of recent major conflicts. Some clergy are good at coping with conflict; some are not. It is a major dumb thing to call a pastor and then thrust this trusting soul into an ongoing conflict. Unfortunately, this kind of mistake happens regularly. An alert search committee can present a recent conflict in a positive light by demonstrating what the congregation learned from the experience. If the church shows a positive trajectory of self-understanding, this is a plus in attracting the right pastor. Most clergy read enough of these profiles to smell a rat by what is *not* said. This particularly delicate matter is one more reason to get professional help in the search process.

Wrong Calls

Besides not doing their homework properly and omitting critical information from the profile, search committees sometimes try to short-circuit the process in one of several ways—with often-catastrophic results. A common error is to call a pastor who is already known to them but who is an inappropriate candidate. At the top of this list is the interim pastor. Congregations often fall in love with a seemingly available interim pastor and wonder why they simply cannot call him or her. There are several reasons not to. First, the chances are excellent that at least one and probably several individuals do not like the interim pastor and will feel disenfranchised by such a call. These folks may not be very vocal because the cultural climate of the congregation simply won't support their negative feelings; however, once the call is made to the interim pastor, the disgruntled members may do whatever they can to cripple the new pastor. Another reason not to call the interim pastor is that sometimes a congregation mistakes their attraction to the interim pastor for love, when it is really infatuation. When the interim pastor becomes the "settled" pastor, he should take up a new agenda. It is entirely possible that while he was a terrific interim pastor, he is not qualified to cope with the particular long-term needs of the congregation. Having said all of this, I hasten to add that sometimes the interim pastor does make a good "settled" pastor; however, most denominational judicatories have a strict policy prohibiting this practice because the track record is generally poor.

Next on the list of dumb calls is elevating an existing assistant pastor into the vacant senior pastor position. In another era, clergy picked their own successors in this way. First, the senior pastor would train the assistant in the details of the job and inculcate him (this was generally before female clergy) in the culture of the congregation, thereby fostering a seamless transition. The problem was that not only was the transition seamless, there was no opportunity for any creative change in the organization. In that earlier time when contextual changes were much slower, there was some justification for this procedure; those days are long gone.

Other clergy on the list of inappropriate, or at least questionable, calls include the search consultant (that has happened!), a former pastor or an assistant pastor, and the pastor next door. Again, because it is likely that someone already does not think well of the individual, the new pastor starts with her foot in the bucket trying to convince some parishioners of the legitimacy of the call. As a matter of statistical probability and good sense, it is better to call someone unknown to the members of the congregation. There are successful exceptions, but these are few.

Management Style

Most parish profiles written for the search process include minor variations on the list of basic pastoral skills: preaching, teaching, pastoral visits, church growth, crisis counseling, youth ministry, Christian education. Likewise, many clergy organize their résumés around the same points. Not very many profiles or résumés have statements about management style, although this may be the most import item in assuring a good match. I believe it is the item most likely to lead to friction in the early period of a new pastorate. Churches and their pastors may overcome divergent theological opinions—they may even overcome diverging worship styles—but if the congregation and clergy are in fundamental disagreement about how decisions are made, there will be constant trouble. Churches and clergy alike should work to determine their management styles and preferences and not hesitate to make this information a part of the profile, as well as part of the interview. See chapter 5 for more on this topic.

A dumb thing that churches do is to assume
that if they can just get through the current transition,
they can stop worrying about change.

Confidentiality

Confidentiality has tripped up a few search committees. The problem lies in not understanding the difference between "confidentiality" and "secrecy." "Secrecy" is the withholding of information in order to gain power over another. "Confidentiality" is the withholding of information because revealing the information would be embarrassing or injurious to someone. Sometimes members of a search committee decide that they need to be secretive. They withhold all information from the congregation from day one until they present the finalist or finalists. The search committee needs to keep information about specific potential candidates confidential because release of the information could be injurious to the candidates' congregations. However, committee members need to be as open as possible to the congregation regarding the process and the criteria being used to find the new pastor.

Transition is really the norm in our era. Things change so fast that pastoral transition is minor compared to the enormous changes taking place in our society and in our church. A dumb thing that churches do is to assume that if they can just get through the current transition, they can stop worrying about change.

What to Do about It

• Seek advice about the transition from your judicatory and/or an outside consultant.
• Use the time well. Transition can be a wonderful time in the life of a church in which to consolidate the history and make solid plans for the future.
• If the search for a new pastor will be the responsibility of a search committee, choose one that represents:
  – all age groups,
  – all ethnic groups,
  – new and old members,
  – leaders and faithful followers, and
  – a range of opinions on key issues.
Search committee members must have the time and patience to work hard for the length of time it normally takes to conduct a search in your denomination (usually twelve or more months).
• Remember the four keys to the pastoral search process.
  – The congregation should know who they are.
  – The congregation should know where God is calling them.
  – The pastor should know who he or she is.
  – The pastor should know where God is calling him or her.

8 Resources

Some churches do not honor the resources they have.

Every generous act of giving, with every perfect gift, is from above, coming down from the Father of lights, with whom there is no variation or shadow due to change.
—James 1:17

A lack of abundance or an abundance of riches can be the center of controversy. While the usual problem is the belief that a church has too few assets, churches can also get into trouble when they seem to have too many assets. The real estate, the endowment, and the cash are the assets that are grist for this mill. It is axiomatic in marriage counseling that couples that fight about money are, in fact, fighting about deeper issues. The same is true for churches. So this chapter is not so much about techniques for handling assets as it is about a church's underlying attitudes about those assets.

Attitude Shift

I know from personal experience that one's approach to money is very important. I grew up in an affluent family. My father died when I was in my first year of graduate school and left a substantial amount of money in trusts. My attitude while growing up was that there was always enough money for me if I could articulate a reasonable plan to my father on how to spend it. Once he was gone, however, I became the sole judge of the quality of the plan. After twenty-five years most of the money was gone and I had to develop a new approach. What I mean by "new approach" is not a tinkering with the budget by generating more income or lowering expenses. What I had to do was to devise a financial strategy that acknowledged that God is the ultimate source of whatever we have or will have and that service to God is what we are called to do.

I certainly did not invent this idea. Stewardship experts have been saying something similar since Jesus observed the widow placing her two coins in the treasury. Truly living this attitude on a daily basis is hard. Our society surrounds us more and more with people and products to help us maximize the impact of our resources: get a new mortgage, have another credit card, work the stock exchanges online. The potential for individuals to get into trouble is high. Attitudes, then, may be changed by positive or negative experiences and these attitudes may then be projected onto a church budget.

Four attitudes about resources show up again and again in churches that are struggling. Sometimes these churches are in deep trouble; sometimes they are just drifting without focus. Certainly a church's attitude about money tells a great deal about what is in its soul.

The Lord (or Somebody) Will Provide

Let us first dispense with "somebody." I made reference in the previous chapter to church budgets that included an income item labeled "new pledges." Talk about counting chickens before they hatch and spending money before you have it. Expecting "somebody" to balance the budget puts the wrong kind of pressure on the newcomer committee. The greeters have to see FUTURE PLEDGE every time they welcome a visitor. Evangelism and the budget have become muddled. The purpose of the organization becomes balancing an out-of-whack budget. Don't put your faith in "somebody." Put it in God.

Still, just saying "The Lord will provide" won't balance the budget either. When the devil suggested that Jesus take a swan dive off the top of the temple to show how the angels would come to his rescue, Jesus refused. He recognized a set-up when he saw one. In times of stress, the devil in us whispers in our ear, "The Lord will provide." We leap joyfully off the temple and crash onto the pavement. I am not saying that having faith in God is a waste of time or that prayer is not answered, but there is a fine line between tempting God and trusting God.

The difference is the extent of our own effort. If we have truly done all we can in a given situation, then we need to turn the rest over to God. Even after we have given our best effort, there is still no guarantee that God will provide the rest. Homeless shelters are full of people who tried very hard but the circumstances of their lives pushed them off the temple and the fall was painful. Theologians have argued for centuries over where God is in that kind of pain; I will not even begin to enter that discussion here. For the purposes of wrestling with resources, suffice it to say that pain can teach us something about our limits. Now let us return to the arena of church budgets and take with us the idea that we must wield the sword of discernment and separate what we *can* do from what we *cannot* do, then leave out of the budget that which we cannot do. Anything else is tempting God.

This is not to say that there cannot be some risks in the program that emerge in the budget. A congregation may wish to try a new curriculum that requires additional spending in the Christian education budget. The church approves the expense hoping that the curriculum will attract new families with young children. That's great, but don't put the new pledges from potential families in this year's budget. Pray that you can put them in the budget next year.

Worshiping the Real Estate

As previously noted, I never cease to be amazed by the number of churches of all stripes that put a picture of their church on the front of their Sunday bulletin. If I were a visitor from another planet, I might logically assume that the worshipers were putting a picture of their deity on the cover. While no one would admit that the building is a god, it often is. Real estate can be just another form of idolatry; however, real estate can also be a wonderful tool. The people need to meet somewhere. Are you going to rent or own? As individuals in the United States, many of us want to own the property rather than endlessly pay rent to an absent owner. We want control of the space that is our church community; we want to be able to meet during the week on any night we choose, and so on. The desire for real estate is strong because owning property is a sign of success in our culture as well as because of the practical realities of worshiping communities. It does make a big difference for a congregation to have its own space. Also, the design of the church in the hands of a good architect can make a statement, about worship. Gothic cathedrals, for example, are a wonder of awe-inspiring space. The fact that they were constructed with funds generated by indulgences is problematic. The devil almost always gets in where money is concerned.

The devil gets into our real estate as well. A church that is planning major construction, whether it is a new building or a major remodeling, is probably a church in conflict. All of the issues about the long-range future of the church come into play. Sorting these out can be an exciting and fruitful exercise. Unfortunately, issues of turf also come to the surface. For example, choir members might propose to raise a large chunk of money if they can have control of the design of the music rehearsal room. This happened in one church and the resulting room was designed in such a way that it could not be used for anything other than choir practice. The choir had staked out its territory in the new building.

Consider again the Goodbody Room described in chapter 2. When space was needed for AA meetings, the woman's guild turned the request down saying they didn't want coffee stains on the new carpet.

A look at a church's budget can be very revealing. If the church is spending a huge percentage of the budget for either mortgage payments or for maintenance of its building, then one may well ask what the ministry is about. Perhaps it is a ministry of real estate. If the church is rented out to worthy community groups at little or no cost, one can make a case for saying the real estate is the ministry. However, this is usually a fallback rationalization when pledges drop and the mortgage and maintenance line items become serious problems.

The adage "We don't know what the future holds but we know who holds the future" applies here. Most of the people who built the church buildings we occupy are no longer around. The buildings may or may not serve the needs of the current congregation. It may be very painful to admit this and look at alternatives, including selling the real estate, but good strategic planning and good stewardship demand thinking creatively about all of the assets of the church.

Burning Out the Volunteers

The members are the most important resource a congregation possesses. A church can manage with very little money, no building, and little or no clergy leadership, but there must be people who are willing to apply their spiritual gifts to the work of the church.

The difficulty for the church in coping with all of these talents is organization and commitment. The process of organizing volunteers in the church is a little like herding cats. Possibly that is because the mission is often vague and the strategies diffuse. Consider a different volunteer organization for a moment—a community theater. In a community theater, many different kinds of talents are needed from acting to directing to technical skills to accounting. These are widely divergent talents. Since the mission of the theater is to perform plays, the focus and the job descriptions are clear and usually limited to the length of the run of the play. Consequently, once committed, the volunteers are likely to stay in their jobs for the run of the show. In the church, the show goes on indefinitely and it is not always clear what the show is. One can sign up some volunteers to fold, stamp, and bulk-sort the newsletter and they do it. But who does the next newsletter and the one after that? How long will the same person or family commit to the same job?

The church uses up its volunteers—its talent base—like consumers use paper towels. Church volunteers can be like cannon fodder in a World War I trench. Knowing the talents of your members is not enough. One has to know how and when to draw on these talents. Saint Paul's wonderful description of the Body of Christ as various body parts in 1 Corinthians 12 states that no part is more important than another and that the parts need to work together. Furthermore, the parts need to give each other a break every now and then.

As for commitment, consider again the problem of cutting the grass on the church grounds. Suppose someone volunteered for the job with good intentions, but does not do the job. The lawn looks like a hayfield. Possibly no one else is inclined to do the job so the job does not get done. Then either the wrong people are being recruited as grass cutters or there is a larger problem with volunteer commitment in the church. I have worked with several churches that complained about a lack of commitment on the part of their volunteer youth advisors. In every case I found that the lack of commitment in this area reflected a lack of commitment in other areas.

The problem of volunteer commitment is bound up in some very serious issues, including trust, boundaries of membership in the group, clarity around the mission of the enterprise, and agreement about that mission. If the grass is not getting cut, and the newsletter is not mailed on time, and there are never enough Sunday school teachers, then the church has a serious problem that goes well beyond issues of accountability for volunteers.

Accountability and a business-like approach for volunteers does not require hierarchical schemes; however, a hierarchical structure with lines of accountability may help to insure that the work gets done. The team concept is also important. The pastor and lay leaders may well see themselves as a team and function in that way. Similarly, the grass-cutting crew can see themselves as a team and function that way; furthermore, they are more likely to do so if the church leadership demonstrates the model. Ultimately, the congregation itself is a team; "We are in this together" is the motto for clergy and laity alike.

The Glass Is Half-Empty

Every church board has or should have at least one curmudgeonly member who always says that "it" can't be done because there isn't enough money. The "we can't afford it" person is necessary to the health of the organization as a whole but should not dictate all decisions. Financial decisions need to be based primarily on what a church does have rather than on what it does not have. This may seem like a silly and foolish observation, possibly even an inferior version of "The Lord will provide," but I would claim that building a church budget based on what you have rather than on what you do not have is a critical shift in attitude.

The "glass is half-full" attitude requires some form of faith budgeting combined with zero budgeting. "Zero" means few prior assumptions about what must be funded. Basically, the tactic is to:

- look at the available resources (pledges, other income, real estate, volunteer time and talent);
- look at the church's mission statement and strategic plan for ministry; then,
- plan a ministry that uses these resources to the maximum to carry out the strategic plan.

Stewardship officers of every denomination preach this sermon all the time, but finance committees still resort to in-the-box thinking that assumes that last year's expenses form the backbone for this year's budget.

More than any other institution, the church has the responsibility to think creatively every year about how best to use its
resources. One church I worked with had a substantial endowment that generated about a third of the church's income. The
endowment income was channeled into the operating budget,
which looked rather ordinary in its division of salaries, program,
outreach, and building maintenance. The leaders of the church
knew that there was something wrong with this picture and
wanted help doing some out-of-the-box thinking about how to
use their endowment more creatively. They eventually decided to
channel all of the endowment income into outreach incrementally
over five years. The shift in attitude in that congregation was from
seeing a full glass to seeing an overflowing glass.

Perhaps my years in campus ministry have made me overly
zealous on this point. Campus ministry, which usually has very little in its financial glass, changes with every semester as students
with different needs and talents come and go. There are some constants, but the energy and focus of ministry are always changing.
Therefore, every semester I must look at the resources of money,
time, and talent and put together a new ministry. Likewise, the
energy and focus of parish ministry are also constantly changing,
although the speed may seem to be glacial. Even so, the attitude or
process is the same. Matching up available resources with desirable ministry means the glass is always at least half-full and the
ministry is bound for a lot of success. Let God worry about the
empty part of the glass and that too may be filled.

What to Do about It

It should be clear that the first step in avoiding problems regarding the church's resources is one of attitude: remembering how it
is that we came to have whatever we have. If the staff or members
are troubled by not having the resources they think they need,
they should ask themselves this question: What resources must we
have in order to be a church? They may discover that they have
abundance but that it is a different kind from what they wish for.
Then do this:

- look at the available resources (pledges, other income,
  real estate, volunteer time and talent);
- look at the church's mission statement and strategic plan
  for ministry; then

• plan a ministry that uses these resources to the maximum to carry out the strategic plan.

There is more on this subject in the conclusion.

Regarding volunteers, this is one area where the church can draw on good business practice. The only real difference between a paid employee and a volunteer is the pay. In all other respects, volunteers should be treated with the same respect and mutual accountability as the paid staff. Volunteers need to have a clear contract that states:

1. This is the job.
2. The job will take x hours per month and will last for y months.
3. You are accountable to this staff person.
4. If you can't perform your job, you need to inform the staff person and/or find a substitute.

While these points do not necessarily need to be set forth in writing with a formal job description, they do need to be clearly understood; writing them down may be a good idea in many cases. Consider once more cutting the grass. Since more than one person may volunteer for this job, it is a good idea to have a job description that gives details on how and when the grass is to be cut. The job description could be the basis for some kind of simple contract that further spells out how often the job is to be done, and the length of the contract. (It is much easier to recruit a volunteer if the job does not stretch forward into an infinite future. No one likes to be a quitter, but everyone is a quitter with contracts that lack an end.) A good contract should also contain some points on accountability: the grass cutter reports to the chair of buildings and grounds; the grass cutter is expected to do the work on the agreed-upon day or must call one of the other grass cutters to substitute. This kind of contracting may sound a bit harsh for volunteers in a church, but without good paths of accountability, the grass may not be cut.

Finally, be sure to affirm the volunteers whenever possible. One pastor I know has a commissioning service once a year for everyone who does any volunteer job for the church as well as a celebratory reception for the volunteers at the end of the program year.

# 9 Worship

Some churches offer worship that is not consistent with who they are or where they want to go.

I hate, I despise your festivals, and I take no delight in your solemn assemblies.
—Amos 5:21

What would it be like if there were worship critics in the manner of restaurant, theater, or film critics? The worship critic would attend a different church service each week and print a review in the local newspaper. What criteria would the worship critic use? Possibly we could all agree that in worship we connect with God, but the ways in which we do so vary enormously. One service may emphasize the word while another may emphasize sacrament. Some will maintain that one hour is the right length for a worship service while others will maintain that worship goes on as long as necessary. The posture for prayer varies from kneeling, sitting, and standing to standing and swaying with arms raised. The worship critic would be hard-pressed to evaluate all of the different forms of worship using objective criteria. Furthermore, regarding connecting to God, the worship critic can interpret only his or her own connection with God as experienced in the service. There is no way to know for certain what someone else is experiencing.

I have never been asked to consult with a church about its worship life. There is probably a consultant out there somewhere who will help a congregation select choir robes, rewrite the service sheet, examine the music for key relationships, and possibly critique sermons. It stands to reason that people do not want an outsider tampering with their worship as worship consists largely of references that connect at deep levels to the individuals in the congregation.

Worship is the most visible part of any church and usually the point of entry for newcomers. Therefore, worship is central to the growth of the church. Worship usually consists of some combination of praise, reading of Scripture, interpretation of Scripture, prayer, and, sometimes, sacramental rituals. But every denomination and local church may define, select, design, and use these elements quite differently.

For good or ill, worship is a bubbling theological and aesthetic soup seasoned by the life experiences of the congregation. Scripture, music, pageantry, and oratory all rise to the surface and then recede, only to come around again in their turn. Done well, the soup is an elegant, nourishing blend that can be hearty or light, simple or complex. Done badly, worship is a sickening concoction of ingredients that are far from nourishing. Defining "good" or "bad" worship is an inevitably subjective process.

For example, I have my own biases about worship. I was raised in a large, urban, Episcopal parish in which worship was executed at a high aesthetic level that included an excellent pipe organ, a full-time organist, a paid choir, excellent preaching, a good lighting system, and so on. That was a very rich soup indeed. While I still enjoy and appreciate the kind of worship I first experienced, I also like quiet, meditative events in simple circumstances. As a person who loves good music, theater, and writing, I prefer worship that includes all of these elements and that does them well. But that is just my preference. In congregational worship, what is a mediocre experience for one person may be an epiphany for another. What is inspiring to one may be annoying to another. What is the worship critic to do?

People can tell you immediately if they like or dislike something in worship even if they cannot present a rational reason for their dislike. One new pastor in a church where preaching was central always prefaced her sermons with a transcription from the psalms used by many preachers: "May the words of my mouth and the meditations of our hearts be always acceptable in your sight, O God, our strength and our redeemer." Some in the congregation complained about the "new and unfamiliar" words that the new pastor used to preface her sermons because the previous beloved preacher did not use them. As irrational as the complaint may have been, it was very important to a few people.

As for the theological content of worship, an ecumenical worship critic would have to be very flexible regarding Christology to go from one church to another, not to mention such issues as sacramental theology, the doctrine of the Trinity, and so on. What is left as solid criteria for evaluating worship?

For me the fundamental issue is coherence and connection. Are the various worship elements in harmony with each other? Are the choices made in designing the worship event connected to the hopes and dreams as well as the experiences and traditions of the community? Does anyone connect to God? The dumb thing that churches do is to hold worship events that do not make sense in themselves and do not connect with the life and faith of the worshiping community and the mission of the church. In this dumb worship service, connection to God would be a random accident or a matter of grace, depending upon your theology. Having put forth a lengthy apologia, I now offer a few specific dumb things that can cause trouble.

Change or Freeze?

Changing a congregation's worship precipitously is a very dumb thing indeed. Doing so trifles with some of the deepest places in the hearts of the people. Even those who outwardly appear to have little spiritual content in their lives can be deeply disturbed by changes in their worship life. Good worship is a liminal expe-

> The dumb thing that churches do is to hold
> worship events that do not make sense in
> themselves and do not connect with the life
> and faith of the worshiping community and
> the mission of the church.

rience that connects deeply with people at an emotional, precognitive level. Anyone who has had an experience of the presence of God during a worship event is forever marked by that experience and will want to try to recreate that moment. Christmas provides the clearest example. People who may go to church only rarely will sometimes "get it" at Christmas—that is, they will feel a sense of connection to God. They will go back to the church they grew up in or wherever it was that they "got it" so that they might "get it" again. Or they just go to church somewhere in the hope of recreating that connection.

One church in my experience deliberately played to this reality. They held a "public" service on Christmas Eve at 7:00 P.M. that lasted an hour and was oriented for families that did not usually attend church. The people who came to this service usually wept openly during the singing of "Silent Night." They may have received a genuine annual epiphany or they may have been affected by the whiskey in their eggnog. Nothing about the service ever changed and it was always a huge success.

The same congregation also held a midnight service that they regarded as "their" service. It was subject to more variation in accordance with changes in the worshiping community and ran longer. Since this was a large church in a small town, the leaders saw this twofold strategy as part of their community responsibility, and it worked. Everyone's worship needs were met.

It is reasonable to want to feel some connection to God during worship. While no worship leader or team of leaders would ever dare to guarantee an epiphany, leaders do want to maximize the possibility that it will happen. The church with the two very different Christmas services was simply trying to increase the likelihood of God connections.

Like many other churches of all sizes, this congregation dealt with the weekly Sunday schedule using a similar strategy. They had a quiet 8:00 A.M. service without music, then a 9:00 A.M. service oriented toward young families that contained some contemporary music with guitar accompaniment. At 11:00 A.M. they held a more traditional service that appealed to their older members. When they combined the 9:00 and 11:00 A.M. services during the summer, there was little compromise. They generally followed the more traditional liturgy because it was the least likely to offend anyone.

This pattern can be found in congregations of every denomination in every part of the country. That is because the biggest problem with change in worship is a generational issue. One generation will be attached to a particular combination of music and liturgy and expect to have that same worship experience all of their lives, up to and including their funerals. It is worth noting that members of this older generation usually hold leadership positions and pay most of the bills in the church. Even if they did not hold the power, they still deserve their epiphanies as much as anyone else does. Every generation is important. But there is an obvious problem in trying to match the needs of the older, regular members with the needs of younger members who may not yet be in the church. Which constituency is more likely to have their needs met? Can the church minister to both generations? Should they? What choices are consistent with the strategic plan of the church? To put this problem in business terms, who, where, and what is the market?

In areas with a certain population density, FM radio stations compete fiercely and must make choices similar to those of the churches. These radio stations play "oldies" to narrow, often generational, niche markets. One "oldies" radio station in my town appeals to the same age group year after year. The target age range is absolute, so every year new people come into the lower end of the age group as some advance out the top end. The music mix is always from the target audience's teen years, advancing one year at a time. Presumably, the strategy makes the advertisers happy—the station has been following it for a number of years.

Obviously, if churches followed the radio station's example and kept their liturgy evolving every year, some parishioners would move from church to church every ten years or so to find a comfortable and familiar liturgy. What churches are more likely to do is to "lock in" on a particular mode of worship and stick with it as their congregations age. For instance, one congregation created a very progressive rock mass setting in the early 1970s, when the church was composed of mostly young families. The church still offers essentially the same service today with many of the same families—now grandparents—in attendance.

It is not sensible for a church simply to freeze its entire worship life around the preferences of a particular generation. There is a one hundred percent probability that the people will die off and the church with it. Such a worship service may have integrity in that it connects to the life and faith of the community; however, the "museum" mode of worship is probably not compatible with the mission of the church unless that mission includes something akin to a mutual suicide pact. Amazingly, many churches have frozen worship anyway.

An obstacle for many congregations is the attempt to balance what they feel is the integrity of their traditional worship with a desire to draw in "unchurched" people. If the music and texts are obscure, newcomers may not come back. If there is too much stuff that everyone seems to "know" but which a first-timer cannot figure out, then the visitor feels like a fool. On the other hand, using an overhead projector to splash the hymn texts on the wall may seem undignified to some. Leaders need to make decisions about worship based upon the strategic plans for the church. If church growth is a priority, then the worship must be accessible and not require a juggling act of books and pieces of paper or hidden knowledge about what to do and when to do it.

The church that never changes its worship will almost certainly die. The church that does change its worship risks losing some members and may or may not attract new ones. Dying is not a bad thing; people do it all the time. Risking offending members by making changes is not a bad thing; it is the only way to grow. The important question is: What worship is most consistent with the mission of the church and the strategic plan?

The Christmas Pageant

The Christmas pageant, traditional in many churches, is a potential minefield. All of the forces of the universe, at least those in a typical congregation, are played out in the course of executing the Christmas pageant.

I was planning on a career in drama before I felt the call to ordained ministry, and I have continued to do drama in church. As a result, I have frequently been asked to direct the Christmas pageant. The first time I did so I was a seminary student working at an artistically sophisticated parish in a university town. I rewrote the tired old script, lined up a classmate to help with the costumes, and designed staging that included some simple lighting in the otherwise rather dim church. I circulated the rehearsal schedule and cast the older children who seemed to have some ability in the key roles.

My first lesson was that it is the parents who get the kids to the rehearsals. In order to have cooperation from parents, they must be included in every phase of the planning, especially in the casting. The second lesson was that it was unlikely that anyone would learn any lines. The third lesson was that no one wanted to change the pageant in the first place. I could catalogue lessons four through twenty, but you get the point. The most important lesson was that the Christmas pageant is not about aesthetics.

Churches everywhere do Christmas pageants with bad singing, bad costumes, incomprehensible readings of Scripture, and shepherds wandering about the sanctuary. They produce the same pageant year after year. Why? Because the children, God willing, learn something about the Christmas story by acting it out; probably more to the point, the parents get something out of seeing their children do something "up front" in the church. I have seen some ugly battles between parents who did care about the performance level of the pageant and parents who were content to have a son or daughter just get through the event. These arguments really underline what different people think "praising God" means. I have seen mothers say horrible things abut each other because one mother's daughter was cast as Mary and the other one's daughter was to be Gabriel. These arguments say a lot about the congregation's understanding of what it means to be the Body of Christ, where all parts are regarded as equally important. I have seen a professional musician take on the director over the quality of the performance. I have seen a whole staff argue over whether the pageant should be part of a regular worship service, a special worship service, a presentation in the church, or a presentation in the parish hall. All of these debates bring into play some serious issues that surround worship: What is acceptable for "praising God"? Who is worship for, God or the congregation? And perhaps the thorniest issue of all: Why do we always do it the same way? These are all important considerations for any congregation. Unfortunately, they surface during a time of the year when everyone is overscheduled and somewhat emotional. Worse, the issues are often played out on the heads of children.

The Christmas pageant is not a dumb thing, but it is often heavily freighted with issues that may run deep for individuals or groups in the church. For that reason, the staff and the director of the pageant need to be in full agreement about how the event links to the priorities of the church, then do their best to stay focused on those priorities. Pageants that run away from the values of the congregation can ruin everyone's Christmas.

The Worship Committee

As a congregation evolves over time, the people's hopes, fears, and aesthetic preferences change and need to be taken into account—but how? While churches that do good strategic planning recognize the problem, they may still have some difficulty finding a solution.

Some churches institutionalize the decision-making process in a worship committee; however, the structure, membership, and procedures of worship committees vary significantly. Some worship committees are strictly mechanical and consist of the functional leaders of worship: head usher, coordinator of readers, altar guild, and so on. Other worship committees include the music director, the Christian education director, and the pastor; together, they actually design worship services. As with other areas of management, the polity, tradition, and the particular gifts of the pastor and other staff members will determine how decisions are made around worship. The difficulty is that many people in the congregation have the same attitude about worship that they have about restaurants: if they just had a chance, they are certain they could manage it better than the professionals. The question, then, is how much access does the congregation have to the decision-making process for worship? A serious mistake is for church leaders to delude themselves into thinking that they have an open system when, in fact, they have a closed system.

I suspect that many church professionals, although they might not admit this publicly, would like to plan and carry out the worship "their" way, with as little interference as possible. Consulting with a team of well-meaning nonprofessionals takes time and often leads to worship that looks like it was designed by a committee. Still, if the management style of the church is one that favors collaboration and consensus, then the staff will be under some pressure to consult with the worship committee regularly or risk steady conflict. Staff can and often do torpedo worship committees by recommending dull people to serve, by letting the committee members endlessly debate trivia such as the format for the service sheet, or by simply ignoring them.

Obviously, the community must have some input to the worship service, even if it is only indirect input through the pastor's spouse. If this is so obvious, why, then, does decision making around worship often become such a problem?

Since worship is to some degree an artistic event as well as a teaching, praising, praying, and sacramental event, problems in worship planning are often disputes between the aestheticians and the theologians. The chief aesthetician of any church is usually the

musician. He or she naturally draws into the choir other aestheticians or wanna-be aestheticians. Since they regard themselves
(possibly correctly) as the only people on the premises who have
any appreciation for the drama of the liturgy, the mystery of the
sacraments, and the power of the music, they are most likely to be
the people in the congregation who complain about worship. An
extraordinary amount of church conflict begins right at this dark
intersection. Negative feelings about the pastor can find their first
expression in the back channels of conversation as singers head for
home after choir practice. The aesthetically challenged pastor or
the theologically challenged musician who does not nurture a
good working relationship with the other will need to check his or
her back regularly.

Arrogance

Arrogance on the part of a congregation about their worship is
the dumbest thing of all. My own Episcopal branch of the faith
probably has more than its share of offenders, but there are
plenty of arrogant congregations of all denominations. I am talking about a church whose members think that their worship is
just the most wonderful thing on earth; and if others would just
come and experience it, they would fall over each other becoming
pledging members.

Episcopalians fall into this trap because they have such a high
regard for aesthetics and sacramental worship. For other congregations it may be their theology. There are liberal churches so
impressed by their use of inclusive language and the ethnic diversity of their music that they are confident that anyone would feel
so welcomed by their church that they would never leave once they
got in the door. In all of these examples, the congregations claim
evangelism just by having such wonderful worship. Worship may
be an essential element in evangelism, but it is not the only one.

Noise during the Service

Noise generated by children can be an especially difficult issue for
the church with only one main service coupled with a desire to
have young families as a part of the worshiping congregation. The
liberal concept of inclusion collides with legitimate concerns for
dignity, aesthetics, and the spiritual ambience of worship. The

solutions range from segregating the noisy families by holding their worship services at separate times or in separate spaces, placing the children in their own worship event or activity, or letting go of the matter. All of these solutions have some cost in personnel time, physical remodeling, or general happiness. The larger issue of the role of children in worship raises a host of collateral issues—from "family values" to the purpose of worship. I have seen this issue fester in a number of churches, causing tension for everyone in the worship space, from the parents of the noisy children to the adults who demand silence. A failure to decide this issue is probably a failure to have a clear sense of identity and/or call (see chapter 6). In some churches the congregation and staff have made a choice, but no one is willing or able to say "no" to whoever needs to hear it (chapter 3).

Ultimately, worship is both a personal and corporate event. Consequently, creating a worship service that includes everyone's needs is difficult, if not impossible. However, if the congregation has unity around its godly mission and strategies, the task of constructing and engaging in worship for the community can be a joy.

What to Do about It

Worship is the one area of the church that is most likely to include activities that fall into the category of "We always did it this way." While it may be a tedious process, try looking objectively at every phase of the experience from "car door slam" on arrival to "car door slam" on departure. Ask these questions:

- What is the function of worship in your congregation (inspiration, education, praise, use of sacraments, and so on)?
- Is your church offering the experience that you want your current members to have?
- Is the experience conducive to drawing and holding new members whose previous worship experience may be quite different? Is that important?
- Does the worship plan conform to the strategic plan?
- Does your worship meet the aesthetic expectations of the congregation?
- Is there a clear policy on the role of children in worship?
- Does the worship have some unifying thread through the use of text, music, or some other element?

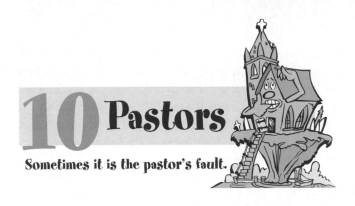

10 Pastors

Sometimes it is the pastor's fault.

My people have been lost sheep; their shepherds have led them astray, turning them away on the mountains; from mountain to hill they have gone, they have forgotten their fold.
–Jeremiah 50:6

Whenever there is a problem in a church, the pastor is usually fingered as the person behind the problem. After all, he or she is the "chief executive officer." If there is a problem, he should know about it. If there is a mistake in the Sunday bulletin, she should have caught it before it was printed. Never mind the fact that the pastor is not a mind reader and does not have unending amounts of time to devote to the job. The principle of "the buck stops here" is a powerful one in business, government, and the church. When a baseball team goes into an extended slump, the owner will eventually replace the manager, even though the manager is not the person swinging the bat. But sometimes it is the manager's fault, the CEO's fault, the president's fault or the pastor's fault. Sometimes the problem is a subtle issue of leadership style and sometimes it is gross mismanagement. Lay people who think they can skip this chapter should at least look at the section headings. If any of these problems sound familiar, you can help your church by sharpening your understanding of what is going on with your pastor.

Changing Too Much Too Soon Too Fast

Just as there are two ways to remove a bandage, there are two schools of thought on how to bring about change in a new pastorate. Either you can rip the bandage off and absorb all of the pain at once, or you can spread out the pain by pulling very slowly on the bandage. It may be true that the ripping method incurs the same amount of pain, but because it takes less time to execute, it is soon forgotten. The problem with translating this analogy to a church is the last point. In most churches, nothing is soon forgotten or forgiven.

We have already looked at change in some detail in previous chapters. There is no question that institutions resist change and churches can be among the most resistant of all institutions. For this reason, if no other, new pastors should make changes only after building trust within the congregation. Most pastors who change things early in a new pastorate have good intentions. They may even feel that they were called to a particular place because their particular skills were needed in that place, so they assume a mandate for change. They change the worship to include guitars, fire the beloved but incompetent church secretary of twenty years, and spend ten thousand dollars on a new logo—all within the first three months. Changes like these without careful preparation are like flashing a red cape in front of a bull. One study has shown that the median number of pastors who leave a church under some form of duress do so in the first eighteen months of their pastorates.[8] One could infer that some early attempts at change met with significant resistance.

Ultimately, coping with change is coping with fear (see chapter 1). Love, trust, and knowledge drive out fear, so good communication is the starting point in breaking down resistance to change. The pastor needs to do a lot of listening early on and to continue that listening. Parishioners need to feel that they have been heard even if the pastor holds a different point of view. One prominent pastor delivered strongly worded sermons against the war in Vietnam long before it became fashionable to do so. When asked how he kept the long-time pledgers in the fold, he said that before delivering a potentially controversial sermon, he would tell the "little old lady" lobby what he was going to do and solicit their responses in advance. They disagreed with him and told him so; however, they were willing to follow where he led because he took the time to seek them out and listen. They did not agree with him, but they did not cut their pledges or stop coming to church.

Listening, then, does not mean doing only what the members want. I knew a restaurant owner who thrived on repeat business and cultivated his regular customers. One of his tools was a large diary kept at the reservation desk. People who go to nice restaurants frequently have an opinion or two on how to improve the restaurant—different salt shakers, different desserts, and so on. This particular restaurant owner would graciously stand by the door as people left. Usually they would tell him how wonderful the meal had been and sometimes offer a suggestion. He would listen attentively and tell the customer what a wonderful idea it was and, while the customer was watching, write it down in the diary. In fact, he wrote down little in the diary and rarely consulted it. Nevertheless, he was very successful in the restaurant business and had enough shrewdness to change his menu and decor as people's tastes changed over time. He always listened to his customers, but he only used suggestions that he was convinced would improve his business. The point is that there are times to lead the sheep and times to follow the sheep.

Even with good listening skills, a new pastor may blunder his or her way into unwittingly tampering with a cherished tradition. I witnessed a gifted interim pastor who stumbled over one of these land mines. With the aid of the janitor, he moved the pew that stood at the very back of the church. He did this to facilitate the movement of the choir before and after the service. The next Sunday he discovered that someone had returned the pew to its place—a serious task since it was a large, heavy oak pew. After the service, the interim pastor and the janitor again moved the pew out. The next Sunday it was back in its original position. This time the interim pastor asked the head usher if he knew who had moved the pew back. The head usher, who was also a prominent, long-time leader in the church, said that he and the other ushers had moved it back under his direction. When the interim pastor asked why, the head usher explained that it was Mrs. Goodbody's pew. The interim pastor, who had been in this particular church for over six months, asked who Mrs. Goodbody was. The usher said that she was an elderly woman who came to church once every other month or so and always sat in that pew, and that she would be terribly upset to find that her pew was missing. (Ironically, this church was founded in the late 1800s as a reaction to pew rent and pew ownership.) The pew remained in the church.

There is no way a new pastor is going to know all of the hidden land mines of tradition lurking in a congregation. Often the congregation does not know what they are until something or someone happens to bring them to the light of day—such as someone trying to move the furniture. When something like this happens, the pastor is painted with an ugly brush that colors him arrogant and insensitive. The colors are difficult to supplant.

A new pastor will inevitably trip one of the land mines. How he or she handles the situation will be important in establishing authority while also showing respect for the traditions of the congregation. Deliberately tripping land mines is foolish without careful planning.

Weak or Mismatched Management Skills

A subtle way that new pastors work their way into early difficulty is by not grasping the management style of the congregation as described in chapter 4. Ideally, the search committee knows what kind of management style works well in their church and issues a call accordingly. Of course, that assumes that the necessary reflective work has been done and done well by both pastor and search committee—a major assumption. When it is not done, the church's expectations—either overt or covert—are not met and there is conflict. (See chapter 9 for more on this problem.)

Gross mismanagement is another matter. Large, obvious mistakes from mishandling the staff to offending the women's prayer group by ignoring them at the annual meeting are correctable errors. A pastor can be trained to manage staff effectively and can learn to be more sensitive to the various constituencies in the congregation. Pastors with no ability to learn on the job should consider a different line of work. There is no standard instruction manual that covers every situation in pastoral ministry.

Bad Cultural Mix

There can be a successful mixing of cultures of clergy and congregation, but they do not always work. For example, ethnic diversity between staff and parishioners must be exercised with care. An Anglo leading a Latino congregation had better be fluent in Spanish and know something about the traditions of the people he or she is working with.

Although we would like to believe that class background is not an issue in our democratic society, it is a factor. A blue-collar congregation has a particular culture that is different from a white-collar congregation. The pastor needs to be conversant with the culture in which he or she is placed, even if he or she is from a different culture.

Another cultural division that often grates on clergy is in the area of creativity. Many clergy are artists of some sort—writers, painters, sculptors, or musicians; or they may have the kind of creative streak in them that generates new ideas. The creative pastor—whether that creativity is expressed in entrepreneurial or artistic forms—needs to have a forum for expression. While the forum does not necessarily have to be in the life of the church, it is good to be aware of one's expectations and needs.

I knew a pastor whose wife was an artist and a brilliant interior decorator. The couple invited members of the congregation over to their home for events, sometimes in small groups and sometimes for large receptions. Everyone had a good time eyeing the paintings and objects in their home. Unfortunately, hardly anyone in the congregation felt that their homes were remotely interesting by comparison, so they never invited the pastor and his wife to dinner. This reduced the pastor's effectiveness in that congregation because he rarely saw his parishioners in strictly social situations.

Many other cultural issues can divide a pastor and congregation, from what books they read to political preferences. While we can make a case for the value of diversity, diversity does not always work. An Anglo congregation might benefit from having an African American pastor, but would an African American congregation benefit from having an Anglo pastor? In the political arena, consider this question: Would a congregation that does not support the ordination of women benefit from having a female assistant pastor? At what cost? As usual, it takes a lot of wisdom to know what can and cannot be changed.

Genuine Pathology

Finally, consider pastors who exhibit pathological behavior: alcoholism or drug addiction, sexual or physical abuse, bouts of rage or depression. When serious psychological problems exist, the church must act lovingly and firmly to separate the pastor from the church either temporarily or permanently. Sometimes these psychological diseases will manifest themselves in other inappropriate behavior such as conducting a messy affair with a staff member or parishioner. All of these types of problems can cause enormous damage to a parish. The inappropriate behavior challenges the church members' sense of loyalty to and trust in their pastor.

Retiring in Place

Most clergy are hard workers. Nevertheless, like everyone else they usually start to slow down at some point. The vigorous man or woman of fifty may have some health problems at sixty that require a different pace, even though the job is the same if not more demanding. This change in energy, while natural, means that something is not getting done that was getting done before, unless staff and volunteers take up more and more of the slack. Some clergy find this to be a terrific perquisite that they may well deserve. In the worst cases, some clergy essentially retire in place, spending more and more time on the golf course and recycling their old sermons. These usually beloved pastors do more harm than they know because the whole parish may slide into sloth.

Although we may expect our clergy to be saintly and have a special relationship with God, they are human beings with the same appetites as everyone else. Congregations routinely place a lot of trust in their pastors and project on them a high level of integrity whether they deserve it or not. It is not surprising, then, that when the pastor engages in some sort of taboo behavior, the whole congregation feels shame and degradation. Some members of the congregation will want to forgive the pastor and some may want to punish the pastor. Whether the pastor is reconciled to the congregation or departs, the wound remains. The wound is greatest if the pastor is run out of town by a posse made up of vengeful church members—or if it *looks* like that is what happened. Handling the exit of a pastor who violated or allegedly violated a taboo is a delicate matter. Congregations and judicatories that do not handle this well pour gasoline on the fire the errant pastor started. Fortunately, some judicatories now have good processes for dealing with these types of occurrences. Congregations should give their denominational executives and consultants the time they need to work through the problem.

What to Do about It

If you are a pastor:

- join a collegial group;
- keep good spiritual discipline; and
- when you need to, seek help from colleagues, judicatory staff, or professional counselors.

If you are a layperson:

- Talk to your pastor; tell the truth in love.
- If that does not work, talk to your lay leaders.
- If that does not work, talk to your judicatory staff.

Conclusion

Our fallibility makes it a sure thing that our churches will do dumb things. Although each of the previous chapters has some specific remedies, here are some additional general approaches for the cure and prevention of dumb things.

Cure

Diagnosis

When Jesus healed the Gerasene demoniac (Mark 5:1–13), he asked the unclean spirit, "What is your name?" The spirit said, "My name is Legion, for we are many." This naming process is the first step in curing any ailment, physical, mental, or spiritual. In the story Jesus permits the unclean spirits to leave the man and enter a herd of swine that then runs over a cliff and drowns in the sea. It would be wonderful if healing were always that simple, but herds of swine and sea cliffs are limited commodities; worst of all, the dumb things done by churches sometimes turn the churches themselves into a herd of swine that rush about frantically. As with the Gerasene demoniac, the demons in the church are often legion. Future book titles could include: *Ten More Dumb Things Churches Do, Still Another Ten Dumb Things Churches Do,* and *Ten Dumb Things This One Church Alone Does.*

Nevertheless, naming the demon or demons is the first step in any cure. A physician will not do much treatment without establishing a diagnosis; otherwise, there is risk of doing the patient more damage. The same is true when diagnosing church ills. I have seen some misdiagnoses that did incredible damage. In one case, a church that was already experiencing some conflict asked the pastor to resign. The denominational judicatory got involved and sent a team of well-intentioned helpers who were trained to deal with issues of substance abuse. Unfortunately, that team had little or no training in the dynamics of conflict or in the particular problem the pastor had, which was only tangentially related to substance abuse. The team was like the hammer that experienced everything as a nail. Consequently, they put the church and the pastor through an inappropriate process for substance abuse; instead of curing their ills, they made a bad situation much worse. Naming the demon *correctly* is always the first step.

A far more common reason for a misdiagnosis is that the person making the diagnosis is also the person with the disease. Jesus addressed this problem in the Sermon on the Mount in the verse about seeing the speck in another's eye while there is a log in one's own eye (Matt. 7:3). Since a church is a system, the life of the church for good or ill is connected to each of its members. People involved in any way in what they think is the dumb thing will find it very difficult to render an objective diagnosis. In most of the anecdotes in the preceding ten chapters, an individual or a group harbored the demon. It is almost a sure bet that those people did not see the problem as being in them. Outside help may be the only way to name the demon in a way that can lead to removing it.

One church suffered a steady parade of trouble of one sort or another. Almost every Sunday the pastoral staff worked hard through the worship service and the adult classes to cope with the issues in the congregation. Nearly every Sunday the pastoral team would go home feeling that they had achieved some success in naming and claiming the demons that permeated the congregation. Then, by noon on Monday, at least one person would have called the church office describing some new crisis: "Mrs. Alpha is angry because Mrs. Beta mumbled when she read the Scripture passage in the service." Believing they could fix the problem, one or another of the pastors would make a point of calling Mrs. Alpha, who would be surprised by all the fuss. It took a while, but eventually the pastoral team learned that most of the crises were in people's heads. This kind of crisis mentality is not in itself serious but may well be a symptom of a deeper demon, and that fact leads us back to the difficulty of diagnosis. With this congregation, what appeared to be curable by the staff was not.

During my childhood interest in surgery, I responded to every proposed malady with the cure, "Cut it out." Simply telling all of the Mrs. Alphas to "cut it out" may not be helpful. Certainly, the art of parish ministry is connected to handling and mediating low-level conflict. Clergy may bemoan that this task can take up a large part of their time and energy and draw them away from what they may see as "real" ministry, but I believe that training and maintaining the congregation is a key part of the ministry. After all, much of the content of Paul's letters to his fledgling churches is about training and maintaining them. Clergy can and should discuss issues in their parishes with other clergy to gain some perspective before performing major surgery; lay people should check with the pastor unless they think the pastor is the problem. In that case, a layperson should talk to the senior warden, the president of the council, or the board. If talking to church leaders is not effective, the layperson should contact the judicatory office.

Treatment

Treating yourself is difficult for the same reason that doing your own diagnosis is problematic. If you have an appendix that needs to come out, you can perform the surgery yourself; however, the procedure will be very painful and the results will be questionable. Performing major surgery by yourself on your congregation may be possible, but you will experience pain in the process and the results will be questionable. While outside help is not necessary in all situations, outside help is likely to be more objective. Furthermore, a consultant or judicatory executive will relieve you of at least some of the personal pain that goes with "telling the truth in love" to people who may not want to hear the truth no matter how much you love them.

In *Moving Your Church through Conflict*,[9] Speed Leas offers a helpful measure of five levels of church conflict:

- Problems to solve—the focus is on the issues.
- Disagreement—there is some personal emotional attachment.
- Contest—it's now a win/lose situation.
- Fight/Flight—focus on hurting the other(s).
- Intractable Situations—take down the church as well.

The dividing line for determining when to call for outside help is at level three. When the personalities in the conflict become more important than the issues, then it is time for that call.

I indicated in chapter 7 that in the case of the pastoral search process, it can make a big difference to get help from someone who is familiar with the search process. There is no shame in asking for help. I have mistakenly tried to fix the plumbing in my home and ended up calling a plumber to repair the damage I caused. Now I just call the plumber; it is less expensive in the long run. Church officers sometimes balk at bringing in outside help when they find out that it might cost them something. Very few churches put money in the budget for hiring consultants. Still, most budgets do contain a line item for church maintenance. If the roof is leaking, the congregation will find the money to repair it. The situation is no less serious when the church system is broken.

Still, there are plenty of occasions where the dumb thing can be fixed internally. For example, the congregation that is operating out of fear rather than love and trust should check its spiritual life—reading the Bible, prayer, and study. A church that has no sense of purpose can develop its own mission statement and strategic plan. Any member of any congregation as well as the staff can improve their ability to be more businesslike by claiming responsibility for commitments and learning when to say "no." A cure that a congregation can perform on its own is similar to the preventative measures that follow. So long as the dumb thing does not include conflict, the congregation probably does not require outside help. If conflict is involved, use Speed Leas's five conflict levels for evaluating when to get help.

Prevention

Just as with physical and spiritual health, prevention is something everyone should do all the time. In the church as well as in individuals, self-knowledge underlies most of the prevention strategies.

Know Who You Are

One summer I took on the responsibility of sailing someone else's sailboat from Florida to Maine. I had lots of time to think about everything that could go wrong, so occasionally I imagined what it would be like to be caught in a severe storm. I contemplated what I would do if the boat began taking on water and what I might cast overboard to keep the boat afloat. I decided that I could discard bunks, cooking equipment, books, supplies, spare parts, and even the anchor, but that I would need to keep the rudder, sail, charts, and some food and water. With those basics, I would still be afloat in the boat and able to make headway.

We can use the same exercise with the church. The church is in trouble; what can we throw out? Must we have a building, professional clergy, committees, worship books, an organ, a computer? Regardless of whether or not the church is in trouble, what must a church absolutely have in order to be a church?

I like to present this exercise at board retreats because it helps to place the issues of the church in perspective. Different branches of the faith and different congregations will answer this survival question a little differently; but, basically, teaching, preaching, and reaching out with the gospel are the elements of the church. We cannot give up the Good News of Jesus Christ and still be the church. The additional good news is that it does not cost a penny to acquire or maintain the gospel. Avoiding doing dumb things begins with the gospel. It is the life jacket on your boat.

By reading the Bible we know that God loves us and that our sins are forgiven. Awareness of salvation is a huge step in establishing the identity of any congregation, but you need to know more. In the previous ten chapters, I stated repeatedly that a lack of self-awareness was a common failing. Not knowing or understanding who you are as a congregation can lead to any number of dumb things.

Finally, knowing who you are includes knowing where the points of power are in the church. What individuals or families are respected (or feared) to such a degree that any decision about the life of the congregation must be put to them early in the process? Are these people benign or tyrannical? If they are antagonists like those describe in chapter 3, who will confront them? Knowing who you are includes these very practical issues that cannot be ignored.

Know Where You Are

Certainly knowing where you are is a matter of physical context: the church is at this address in this neighborhood. But there is also a metaphysical context: in the past this church was one kind of congregation, today it is another kind of congregation, and we pray that it will become yet another kind of congregation in the future. Knowing where you are in this sense means having a clear knowledge of history, being honest about who you are now, and prayerfully forming strategies for the future.

Know How You Are

Take the time to reflect on your own spiritual condition in your church. Do you feel that:

- Your soul is nourished?
- Your spiritual goals are fulfilled?
- You are connected to God?
- You are loved by God?

Or do you feel that:

- You are angry with God and/or the other church members?
- Are you constantly sad about conditions in the church?
- Are you disconnected from God?
- Are you burnt out as a participant in the ministry?

If you respond affirmatively to the questions in the second grouping, then make an appointment to see your pastor. Tell him or her the truth about what you are feeling and why. If the problem is in you, the pastor can probably help. If the problem is more systemic and a number of people tell the pastor the same thing,

---

Stay awake, for you do not know when
the next dumb thing may happen.

---

maybe the pastor can work with the other church leaders or seek help. In any case, do not do what the antagonists do—spread rumors and gossip, complain about the pastor or other church leaders behind their backs, withhold your pledge, or exit noisily from the community. Also, do not suffer in silence and do not give up until you feel you have exhausted every possibility. Then, if you must, exit gracefully.

Know Whose You Are

Finally, remember that you are the beloved of the One who commands us to love one another. This one fact makes the church business different from all other businesses. Thanks be to God!

Knowing who, what, where, and whose we are is a fancy way of saying, "Wake up! Stay alert!" When Jesus faced a difficult night in Gethsemane, he asked the disciples to stay awake and pray with him. Of course, they didn't. Our congregations will need to try to do better. The members of the Body of Christ can take turns on the watch, but all of us are responsible for the health of the Body. Stay awake, for you do not know when the next dumb thing may happen.

Notes

1. Charles M. Olsen, *Transforming Church Boards* (Washington, D.C.: Alban Institute, 1995), xiii. "When I named the malady of the church boards the 'D' word (disillusionment), I learned to pause, for everyone had a story to tell! Paradoxically, two of the most frequent complaints were (1) 'It's run just like a business' and (2) 'It's not run enough like a business'! Both expressed dissatisfaction. One camp looked for efficiency models from business, while the other camp sought a whole different way of being [a] board that would draw from the culture of faith communities."

2. Collins, James C., and Porras, Jerry I., "Building Your Company's Vision." *Harvard Business Review*, Sept.–Oct., 1996.

3. Kenneth C. Haugk, *Antagonists in the Church: How to Identify and Deal with Destructive Conflict* (Minneapolis: Augsburg, 1988).

4. I heard this analogy years ago at a workshop given by an addictions counselor. I no longer recall her name, but I have found the analogy to be helpful in explaining the dynamics of an addictive system, whether it is a family or a church.

5. This is loosely based on *The Addictive Organization* by Anne Wilson Schaef and Diane Fassel (San Francisco: Harper & Row, 1988).

6. Arlin Rothauge, *Sizing Up a Congregation for New Member Ministry* (New York: The Episcopal Church Center, n.d.).

7. Roy Oswald, "How to Minister Effectively in Family, Pastoral, Program, and Corporate-Sized Churches," *Action Information* 17, no. 2 (Washington, D.C.: Alban Institute, 1991).

8. Speed Leas's workshop on church conflict, 1993. (Burlington, Calif.; Alban Institute, September 1983).

9. Speed Leas, *Moving Your Church through Conflict* (Washington, D.C.: Alban Institute, 1985), 19–22.